Praise For
The Giving Challenge

"This book will change your life."
-Cami Walker, New York Times Best Selling Author, *29 Gifts*

The Giving Challenge will show you how you can make a difference, without a lot of time or money. In the process you'll learn to lead a richer life.

-Harvey McKinnon, co-author, *The Power of Giving*

The Giving Challenge is not only an individual challenge but a journey that can be taken by the whole family. The stories and challenges will teach your children invaluable lessons and show them it's easy to give.

-Galit Breen, bestselling author of *Kindness Wins*

"We often make giving a complicated topic. But Stephanie makes it seem simple - and attractive! This book helped me think more about showing acts of kindness in my everyday life."

-Jeff Anderson, speaker and bestselling author of
Plastic Donuts, Giving that Delights the Heart of the Father

THE GIVING CHALLENGE

40 Days to a More Generous Life

S T E P H A N I E   L .   J O N E S

WESTBOW
P R E S S®
A DIVISION OF THOMAS NELSON
& ZONDERVAN

Scripture taken from the Holy Bible, NEW INTERNATIONAL VERSION®.
Copyright © 1973, 1978, 1984, 2011 by Biblica, Inc. All rights reserved worldwide.
Used by permission. NEW INTERNATIONAL VERSION® and NIV® are
registered trademarks of Biblica, Inc. Use of either trademark for the offering
of goods or services requires the prior written consent of Biblica US, Inc.

WestBow Press books may be ordered through booksellers or by contacting:

WestBow Press
A Division of Thomas Nelson & Zondervan
1663 Liberty Drive
Bloomington, IN 47403
www.westbowpress.com
1 (866) 928-1240

Because of the dynamic nature of the Internet, any web addresses or
links contained in this book may have changed since publication and
may no longer be valid. The views expressed in this work are solely those
of the author and do not necessarily reflect the views of the publisher,
and the publisher hereby disclaims any responsibility for them.

Any people depicted in stock imagery provided by Thinkstock are models,
and such images are being used for illustrative purposes only.
Certain stock imagery © Thinkstock.

ISBN: 978-1-5127-5264-9 (sc)
ISBN: 978-1-5127-5265-6 (hc)
ISBN: 978-1-5127-5263-2 (e)

Library of Congress Control Number: 2016913382

Print information available on the last page.

WestBow Press rev. date: 12/15/2016

Preach the Gospel always, and if necessary, use words.
—Often attributed to St. Francis of Assisi

To my mother and papa, who taught me the importance of giving.

And to my husband, who supports my daily
giving and my pursuit of *dreaming big.*

I love you all!

Contents

Author's Note..xi

Preface xiii

Day 1: Taking Notice..1

Day 2: Bring Maggie Home...3

Day 3: A Free Ride and an Answered Prayer 8

Day 4: Priceless Pancakes.. 10

Day 5: Whole Hearts and a Half Eaten Pizza.................. 12

Day 6: Frames for a Friend... 15

Day 7: Fun with Fruit 17

Day 8: Blessing on the Other Side of the Door............... 19

Day 9: Dream Big...23

Day 10: Serendipity!..26

Day 11: Miles and Memories..28

Day 12: Cotton Candy and the Pumpkin Show...............30

Day 13: An American Hero 32

Day 14: Giving Away My Birthday Flowers...................... 35

Day 15: Unexpected Friendship..38

Day 16: Letters in the Mail 41

Day 17: Experiencing Chicago 43

Day 18: Pencils and Prayers.. 45

Day 19: The Guardian Bell..48

Day 20: Scouting for Food..50

Day 21: The Right Stuff 52
Day 22: Pamper Night 55
Day 23: A Smile for a Stranger 58
Day 24: Giving Hearts a Hand 60
Day 25: Twenty-Five Years of Sobriety 63
Day 26: Donuts and Garage Doors 65
Day 27: The Least of These 67
Day 28: The Giving Jar 69
Day 29: Between Me and You 71
Day 30: A Visit to the Past 74
Day 31: Coffee Shop, a Painting, and the Bible 76
Day 32: What Can You Do for Brown? 78
Day 33: Shoes Serving a Purpose 80
Day 34: The ROI of Giving™ 82
Day 35: Impact Women's Fund 84
Day 36: An Empty Seat 86
Day 37: Home Sweet Home 89
Day 38: A Card and a Calling 92
Day 39: Make a Difference to Someone Today 94
Day 40: They Call Me Mom 96

Your Turn! Start Giving Today! 98
Will You Take the Challenge? 101
Acknowledgments 103
Resources 105

Author's Note

When I started my giving journey I never intended to write a book.
I immediately wrote some stories, but others were written down
months or years later. All stories are a recollection of my memory
and are true as I remember them.

Preface

Compassion inspires action. Small, positive actions lead to unexpected reactions. These positive actions change lives, one person at a time. Experience has conditioned us to expect the worst from others. The news is full of one bad story after another. We are surprised when a total stranger sees a need, great or simple, and responds. I try to be that stranger, carefully observing my surroundings, listening to the needs of those around me, and taking action. But I haven't always been good at following through. Sure, I've volunteered my time and donated my money, but I didn't necessarily seek out specific opportunities to give to others. Like everyone else's, my life was busy and I focused primarily on myself and the things I needed to get done in a day's work. I stayed in my own lane.

Listening to the tugging of my heartstrings and having the courage to respond to the needs of others has been difficult and challenging throughout my life. Talking to strangers is awkward. Money was something I needed to keep for my own selfish pleasures instead of giving away freely. My possessions were just that—my possessions—and they weren't to be given to others. I had worked hard for those things. I deserved them! However, much of that changed in 2011.

The beginning of that year ascended as the New Year always does: with the anticipation of coming adventures. I had recently read *29 Gifts* by Cami Walker and decided to embark on my own twenty-nine-day gift-giving journey. As I thought about this experience, I wondered if I should plan my daily giving or allow opportunities to present themselves to me. I decided a combination of the two was the way to go, as there is no wrong way to give!

What I didn't realize was giving daily started to rule my thoughts. I couldn't stop seeing opportunities to give and help others. The possibilities were all around—everywhere I went. For more than five hundred days, I gave a gift away every single day. While that may sound like humble bragging, what I found was incredible! This journey made more of a difference in my own life than it did in those to whom I gave. It changed my relationships with my friends and my family. It improved my marriage. It made me more grateful, and I began to understand that *things* don't bring happiness. In fact, I found the opposite to be true; giving away things and having less brings more happiness. I became more patient and took opportunities of standing in line to meet those around me. I became more generous. I was no longer stingy with that dollar in my pocket. If someone needed, I'd give it away. I struggled on sharing this journey and gifts, as I never wanted it to come across as bragging. But I also wanted to get my story out to tell others that giving is simple. Giving will change your life, just like it did mine.

Opportunities to make a difference are all around us and most take little to no money and/or time. A smile to a stranger, a helpful hand, some donated clothing, festive Easter baskets for the children of the local domestic violence shelter, an encouraging text, a bonus tip for the waitress who is working to put herself through college, or a thank-you note to someone that made a difference in your life. These gestures may seem simple, but they *do* make a difference. How do I know? How can I be certain? Because I have done these very things. I have seen smiles and tears; I have received hugs from strangers and witnessed the sense of relief, joy, and happiness of those to whom I've reached out. And for that moment in time, the people I gave to knew someone cared. I believe each simple gift made a difference.

In this little book, I share forty of my favorite gifts I have given, received, or heard about over the past five years during my personal giving journey. This isn't a book to be read in one sitting, but feel free to do so. I encourage you to read one story in the morning before you start your day or in the evening before you go to bed. Let it be of encouragement to you and start making a choice to think of others instead of yourself. Even though I have listed days 1 to 40, you can begin with day 1 or day 30; it doesn't matter. You don't have to go in any particular order. Each story stands on its own.

As you read, be challenged to look for, each and every day, ways to give to others. These opportunities will change your life, and that of others. With each story, I offer you a "Giving Challenge," which is a challenge you can do on that day or save for later. The challenges are ideas to jump-start your mind and get you thinking of actions you can take to make a difference. If the challenge listed doesn't apply to you, follow me on social media for more giving challenges and ideas. I also provided a few lines to journal your thoughts, giving experiences, someone's reaction you want to remember, a blessing, or a prayer request. There is also a "Notes" section in the back to journal, doodle, brainstorm, or jot down future gift giving ideas.

I have one request: for forty days, you seek opportunities to give. I don't care if it's forty days in a row or one day a week for forty weeks. But I want for you to commit right now to making a difference in the lives around you for forty days. I want you to share your commitment with a friend or family member and encourage them to join in on the "Giving Challenge." I'll be praying for you on your journey. I'll be praying that God places in your path people that need to see your smile or hear your words of encouragement. I'll be praying that as you go through this journey, if you are struggling with your marriage, an illness, finances, or self-confidence, focusing on others will provide you the perspective you need to change your life, make a choice to be happy, and be more generous. Now let's get giving!

Day 1: Taking Notice

Strolling through the airport, I passed men in black suits on missions to catch their flights, young ladies wearing heels too high and being more concerned about fashion than comfort, and moms soothing exhausted and hungry babies. I approached my gate with plenty of time to spare. I spotted an empty rocking chair, plopped my bag on the ground, and eased into the chair, grateful to catch my breath. I bent over to pull a book out of my bag and caught a glimpse of a young lady sitting a few chairs down from me. Her sobs gave away her heart; she was grieving. I felt a familiar tug on my heart nudging me to approach her and offer help. My first response to myself was not to, but the tugging wouldn't let up, and a feeling of guilt began weaving its way through my body. Hesitating, I rose from the chair and slowly approached the woman. I knelt down next to her and, softly speaking, said, "Hello. Sorry to bother, but are you okay?"

Sobbing, she gasped, "No!"

I asked gently, "Is there anything I can do to help?"

She replied, "No. I'm supposed to be flying to live with my boyfriend, and he just broke up with me. I'm stranded in the airport and don't know where to go. I'll figure it out."

I said, "I'm so sorry. Are you sure I can't help?"

With a slight smile, she answered back, "I'm sure. But ma'am, thank you very much for your concern."

Touching her knee, I replied, "You are welcome."

I returned to my chair and tried to read, but I couldn't stop thinking about this young woman and the journey she was about to embark upon. Time passed by and the next thing I knew, my flight was boarding. As I walked to the line, the young lady called to me, "Ma'am, thanks again!"

Whenever I'm in an airport, I often think back to that moment. Even though she turned down my assistance, I realized my gift wasn't the assistance itself; it was *offering* assistance. It was showing concern to another human being who was obviously troubled. From my rocking chair, I witnessed hundreds of people passing this young lady, and not one person stopped.

Gift giving while traveling has pushed me outside my comfort zone on more than one occasion, usually because the gift giving was to a stranger. Approaching strangers is uncomfortable. If you struggle with the thought of giving to strangers, put yourself in their shoes and ask yourself, "If I needed help, would I appreciate the kindness of a stranger?" If you answered yes, you know what you need to do the next time you encounter a stranger in need. Giving to strangers will stretch you more than you can imagine.

Giving Challenge

Look for opportunities to help strangers in distress. If the tugging on your heart won't let up, reach out and offer assistance. You and the stranger were meant to cross paths.

_____

_____

_____

_____

_____

Day 2: Bring Maggie Home

It's funny how people come and go in and out of our lives. Many times people come into our lives and we have no idea why they are there. Sometimes people exit our lives and we no longer have contact. Other times we lose contact with people and then for one reason we are reacquainted. I always feel God reconnects people for a reason.

I met Matt at Taylor University. He was a friend of a friend, and over the course of our college years, we became friends. After college, Matt and I went our separate ways and wouldn't reconnect until years later through Facebook. Oh, how I love Facebook! Although some people use it inappropriately, you can use it for good to encourage others to give, be positive, dream big, and—most importantly— connect and reconnect with friends.

In June 2011, I started to read the blog of Matt's wife, Shari. Here are bits and pieces Shari shared from her journal from the prior months. I've condensed for the purpose of the book, but check out her blog for the entire story (www.mattsharimaggie.blogspot.com).

* * *

March 18, 2011

I [Shari] went to get a massage. The lady giving the massage came in with her clipboard, and her name was on the back: Maggie. As soon as I read her name, the Lord spoke to my spirit, plain as day. "Yep! You're gonna have a Maggie some day!"

To this, I replied to the Lord (in my head), *Ummm, no. No I'm not.*

Again, the Lord said, "Yep! You're gonna have a Maggie some day!"

Within the next week, God would use people to speak to me. A friend at the play school told me that Matt and I just needed to have another little girl. Another asked me, "Who is Maggie?" That ended up being a worker at the church, but that froze my heart. I told another friend about it—that maybe I made it up in my mind. But she told me, "No. God often prepares us for another season slowly."

May 18, 2011

Another prick. My stomach is in knots. A little guy at the church, Baylor, was wearing a T-shirt that said, "I still live with my parents." I started laughing and said, "Baylor, you still live with Mommy and Daddy?" And, once again, the Lord's voice in my spirit said, *Maggie doesn't live with her parents yet.*

Wow. I wasn't expecting that. The next several hours I was consumed with thoughts of adoption—total fear. Even anger. This is not what I foresaw in our future. But it's not about us, is it? My life is to be for God's glory.

I told my friend Laura about this prick. She told me my and Matt's journey stays with her heart—that she prays for us often. Hmm.

I talked to my friend Kay about sensing the call to adopt and how I wasn't *feeling* gung-ho about it. She said, "Yeah, but I don't think we have to feel gung-ho about something to obey." Yet another wise woman.

When I am afraid,
I will trust in you.

—Psalm 56:3

Journal Entry

At this point, Matt is willing to go down this road as long as Jesus makes it 100 percent clear—and me too. I'm just not sure how He is going to *convince* us that this is what He sees for our family.

May 29, 2011

I text my friend Jaclyn to see if I could pick her brain about adoption. I told her that God had placed a little girl named Maggie on our hearts. We just didn't know where she was or where to start.

May 30, 2011—8:41 a.m.

Jaclyn texts: "Hey, what age u thinking about adopting? Baby or big kid?"

I told her younger than Jaydn, so between one and five years old.

May 30, 2011—10:02 a.m.

Jaclyn texts: "My agency has a one-year-old on their list named MAGGIE (in China). She is available & adorable!"

May 30, 2011—2:33 p.m.

Jaclyn ran into a friend at the pool. Ends up she has been praying for a family looking into adoption—trying to find their Maggie. Her friend Laura had asked her to pray, and she said she had been praying and praying for us to find our Maggie. Wow.

By day's end, we had pictures and video of our newest daughter, Maggie. Our daughter. Two months ago, I had no interest in another child in our home. Today, I can't imagine not going to get her to bring her home. Only God could change a heart like that. Only God could orchestrate a journey like this. All glory goes to God—and no other. Friday we mailed our preapproval application to adopt Maggie. My heart is so excited!

* * *

If you have adopted a child or know someone who has, you are aware of the financial resources needed to give a child a forever home. Struggling with infertility for years, my husband and I often discussed adopting a child of our own. We were so touched by Shari's words that we made a contribution to the Bring Maggie Home fund.

I later received a short note from Matt.

> Hey, ma'am, I just wanted to send you a quick thank-you for your donation to Bring Maggie Home. Because of it, we were able to send out our I-800A, which is the application for approval for Maggie's US citizenship! We really appreciate your and Mike's generosity.

After Shari and Matt were officially Maggie's parents, we received another thank-you note with Maggie's picture. Opening the card and seeing her little face, tears streamed down my face. It was amazing that friends, family, and strangers all came together to bring Maggie home.

That is the power of giving.

Giving Challenge

Do you have friends involved in the adoption process? Ask them how you can help. If you don't know anyone personally, check out my resources section for several great agencies that assist families with adoption.

_____

_____

_____

_____

_____

Day 3: A Free Ride and an Answered Prayer

It's amazing what happens when we strike up a conversation with a stranger.

This is a story about Don, my driver to the airport. I quickly learned he started his own chauffeur business two years ago and hasn't looked back.

At one point in our conversation, he said, "You should write a book!"

I chuckled and said, "I am. It's about giving."

We proceeded to chat on several other topics, and when he pulled up to let me out, he said, "You know what? I'm not charging you for your ride today. My gift."

I really appreciated this gift, and not for the reasons you might think. You see, on the way to the airport, I realized that I didn't have enough cash to pay him. I was praying about the conversation I was going to have with him once I got to the airport. I rehearsed my plan in my head. I would give him my business card, take down his address, and promise I'd mail him the money and more for the inconvenience.

I didn't have to have the conversation because God answered my prayer by tugging on the heartstrings of Don.

If you are ever in DC, use Don from Capital Buddy Limo. I can't wait to get back to DC to give my new friend a big hug!

Giving Challenge

Do you own a small business? Every now and then I encourage you to give away your product or service for free. You never know; your act of kindness may end up in a book!

_____

_____

_____

_____

_____

Day 4: Priceless Pancakes

When I was a member of Kiwanis, I had the opportunity to volunteer at the annual pancake breakfast. We had to sell tickets and this request brought memories back of selling wrapping paper and magazines in high school, which wasn't something I wanted to relive. I bought all of my tickets with the intent of offering them to friends and strangers. I thought about who could use the tickets and concluded busy families. I mailed tickets to friends who are always on the go.

Besides giving away tickets, I volunteered to take tickets at the door. Interacting with people from the community made the time fly by. Even though I had given tickets to friends, I still had eleven to give away. While taking tickets, every so often, as a person was reaching for their wallet, I would say, "Keep your money." and gave them a free ticket.

The expressions I received were priceless. Some were shocked, many smiled, and others thought I was joking, but all were very appreciative. I didn't tell anyone the tickets were from me and that made the giving more enjoyable. I believe it isn't the gift that matters or the person who gave the gift; it is the impact the gift has on another person's life. Whether big or small, it will almost always make a difference.

Giving Challenge

Next time there is a pancake breakfast, chili cook-off, or turkey dinner in your community, buy a ticket or two and give them away.

_____

_____

_____

_____

_____

Day 5: Whole Hearts and a Half Eaten Pizza

My husband and I travel often and he always loves to seek out local breweries. On a trip to Niagara Falls, Canada, we located Taps Brewing Company and decided to check off our to-do list "visiting the local brewery." Taps was established in 2004 and brews custom crafted beer in small batches, using only four ingredients: pure filtered water, select hops, choice malted barley, and yeast. Interesting stuff, for beer connoisseurs.

I ordered a personal pizza that I found to be much larger than I had anticipated. As I was eating my first slice, three young adults slid into the booth attached to ours. The first thought that came to my mind was they looked like vagabonds—scruffy-looking with large backpacks. I also noticed how they stared at my pizza then looked at the menu for quite some time. I'm not sure if they were indecisive or they didn't have much money and needed to figure out what they could afford. These were simply my observations; I really had no idea what their story was.

Prior to the pizza arriving, I had downed half a plate of loaded nachos, so after two pieces of pizza, I was stuffed! Leaning over to my husband, I said, "I would love to give the rest of my pizza to the kids next to us as my gift of the day. Is that strange?"

Shaking his head, he said, "No, I think you should do it."

Nervously giggling, I said, "I feel dumb offering a half-eaten pizza. Is that gross? Plus I'm embarrassed. It's always so awkward striking up a conversation with strangers."

"You are always talking about befriending strangers and challenging others to do so. Kind of hypocritical, if you ask me."

He was right! Guilt poured over me and I knew what I had to do. Even though I was initially uncomfortable, I had gotten in the habit of striking up conversations with strangers as a way to make a connection and show kindness. In the middle of our conversation, our sweet waitress, Victoria, came to our table and asked if I needed a box. It was my time! I sheepishly said no, leaned forward, and whispered, "I would really like to offer the pizza to the table next to us."

Victoria smiled and said, "That is awesome! Tomorrow is Thanksgiving in Canada and I can't wait to go to church tonight and share this story."

As we were chatting, I pulled out my wallet, retrieved a "Pay It Forward in Memory of Emily Huntington" card, and handed it to Victoria. I explained how Emily, a high school senior, captain of her basketball team, and soon to be valedictorian, was killed while texting and driving. I shared that her family created the cards as a way to honor Emily's life, keep her memory alive, and challenge others to pay it forward and share her tragic story of the consequences of texting and driving.

Victoria looked at the card, read it over, and said, "I'm sharing this with my brother. He needs to hear this!"

After tucking the card in her pocket, Victoria announced to the table next to us, "This kind lady would like to give you the remainder of her pizza. She has only eaten two pieces, is staying at a local bed-and-breakfast with no refrigerator, and doesn't want it to go to waste. Would you like it?"

Like children on Christmas morning, their eyes lit up and all three nodded eagerly. Victoria picked up the pizza stand and moved it to their table. They devoured it before we even left the restaurant.

I know it sounds silly, but as I write this story, I tear up because like many other times through this journey, I felt a tug on my heart that day. I observed my surrounding and felt called to share my pizza. In these instances, I can never explain why, but I feel like God placed me in their path to help them out, to feed them, to show them kindness, and to spread Emily's message in another country.

We never know the impact of our actions. But there will never be an impact if we never *choose* to take action.

I think about this day and wonder, "Was there a ripple effect?" In some small way, did these young adults pay it forward? Did Victoria share with others Emily's message and how a lady gave away her half-eaten pizza? Was a life saved? Did it cause anyone else to pay it forward? I'll never know the answers to these questions, and for me they aren't the reason why I give. But I do hope that for one small moment in time, strangers connected, food wasn't wasted, and Emily's story was shared.

Giving Challenge

When you have the power to give, how can you pay it forward? How can your small gesture of kindness make a great impact on another person? Honor Emily's memory and don't text and drive. I challenge you to pay it forward and share Emily's story.

Day 6: Frames for a Friend

I'm constantly on a mission to simplify my home and get rid of things that I don't need, use, want, or love. I find myself obsessed with purging; it's a way to lessen stress. During my giving journey, I happened to take down several picture frames from the walls of my house. I stored them in a plastic tote *just in case* I'd need them again for another project.

Several weeks after taking down and storing the photos, a friend of mine mentioned that she needed to purchase new picture frames. Without hesitation I offered her the frames I was storing *just in case*. What is that old saying? "Someone's trash is someone else's treasure?" Please understand my frames were not trash. They were quite nice; I just didn't have a use for them any longer. I delivered the frames to my friend's home, and we were both tickled to death. I was happy to get them out of my house, and she was elated to save a few bucks. It was a fun way to give and repurpose items I no longer needed.

Giving Challenge

What do you own that you don't need, want, love, or use? Is there someone you know who can benefit from these things? I encourage you to give it away! Your generosity will be freeing.

Day 7: Fun with Fruit

I love reading about gift giving! From the Bible to self-help books, we learn and are reminded the more we give, the more we receive. While on this journey, the gifts I've received have far outweighed those I have given. I have gotten to the point where I am not surprised by what I receive; I just smile. Though that's not the reason I give; it is a mere benefit of giving.

I was sitting in my office, for what seemed to be hours on end, when I heard the doorbell ring. Finally! An excuse to leave my office. I scurried down the stairs and saw bright colors shining through the window. I opened the door to find an Edible Arrangements deliveryman with a generous-sized basket filled with pineapple, strawberries, and several varieties of melons and grapes.

One of my favorite snacks is fresh fruit, and Edible Arrangements baskets always have the freshest and yummiest fruit. This basket was the exact pick-me-up I needed, as I had been buried in work with no end in sight.

I read the card and discovered a dear friend had sent me this special treat. As my surprise wore off, I began to think how my husband Mike and I would probably never be able to eat all this fruit ourselves before it spoiled. I hate thinking of food going to waste and knew this was an opportunity to share this gift with others. I got out a disposable container, filled it with fruit, and walked over to my neighbors' house across the street. They were delighted and grateful, and I was happy to see this gift multiply.

Giving Challenge

Sharing our gifts—material, physical, and spiritual—is what we are called to do. I encourage you to share a gift today!

_____

_____

_____

_____

_____

Day 8: Blessing on the Other Side of the Door

I'm thankful for the opportunity to work from home. When I become bored in my office, I set up shop in the kitchen and with a switch in environments, my mood magically changes.

One particular evening, I sat my laptop on the counter and moved all the chairs out of the way so I could practice a training I'd be presenting the following week in Mystic, Connecticut. Yes, home to the famous *Mystic Pizza*, the movie in which Julia Roberts got her start.

As I rehearsed, I heard children laughing outside. Just then the doorbell rang, and I knew it would be neighborhood kids selling something. This gift-giving journey taught me to enjoy the children who came to my door. If I'm being honest, they irritated me before. Do you know the feeling? Perspective is an interesting concept. As they rang the doorbell again, I hesitated to answer the door. Over the past two weeks, I had purchased chicken and potatoes (yes, that's what they sell here in rural Indiana), raffle tickets, and a couple of boxes of chocolates. And then I remembered I still needed to give a gift for day, so I answered the door.

Standing there in front of me were the most adorable blond-haired, blue-eyed boy and girl giggling and smiling. The little girl held a box and the boy had the paperwork. They worked as a team and both did the talking. The little boy explained he was in the Boy Scouts and was selling popcorn. My heart melted as I looked at this little girl helping her friend sell his popcorn. My mind wandered to my childhood and thinking of a time when I had probably gone door to door with my best bud, Kyle, and neighbors looking at us in the same way. I was reminded of all the great neighbors I had growing up that supported us no matter what we were selling. What an encouragement we can be to children who have the courage to ring the doorbell and go for the sale.

Taking the sales sheet and reviewing the list of yummy items, I settled on a bag of cheddar popcorn. I asked if they needed the money that day, and he exclaimed, "Today or tomorrow! But we do take checks! See?" He pulled out and showed me a check that was attached to his paperwork, just in case I wasn't sure what one looked like.

I asked if they would like to step inside while I went and grabbed some money. The little boy replied, "I would love to come in; I've been outside all day." I ran upstairs, grabbed the money, and hurried back down. When I hit the bottom step, the boy exclaimed, "You sure do have a lot of shoe boxes!"

I turned toward my reading room and noticed half the wall filled as high as I could reach with shoeboxes for a project called Operation Christmas Child. The room had looked that way for a couple of weeks, so I'd actually stopped noticing the boxes. I shared with the children that I was collecting shoeboxes to fill with toys and school supplies to send to needy children around the world. The young boy looked up at me and exclaimed an enthusiastic "Cool!"

Without knowing any more about the project, he turned around as if to leave, and said, "I have some toys I could give you for the shoeboxes."

I asked the kids if they wanted to see all the things I had collected for the shoeboxes, and their eyes widened. The young boy immediately blurted out, "Awesome!"

He gently tiptoed to the edge of the room and carefully looked over each pile of items. He picked up a necklace and asked what it said. "Jesus," I answered. He put it back in the box and picked up a bouncy ball, bounced it once, and put it back in the box.

The young girl pointed to a large box and asked if it was filled with crayons. She then said, "I have lots of Barbies. Do you think the children would like to get a Barbie in their shoebox? I could give you some of mine." I said, "I think the children would like that."

The boy then noticed my pile of cars. He said, "I have two boxes full of cars that I don't play with. Do you want them?" I responded, "You don't have to give them to me, but if you want to, that would be nice."

Then Jesus called a little child to Him, set him in the midst of them, and said, "Assuredly, I say to you, unless you are converted and become as little children, you will by no means enter the kingdom of heaven. Therefore whoever humbles himself as this little child is the greatest in the kingdom of heaven. Whoever receives one little child like this in My name receives Me."

—Matthew 18:2-5

As they walked out of the living room, the young boy again took notice of the bucket of colorful bouncy balls and said, "Can I have one?" I smiled and replied, "Yes."

I then asked the little girl if she wanted one too; she nodded, picked up a ball, and placed it in her box. As the boy started to leave, he turned around and said, "Can I have a necklace instead?" "Sure," I replied. He placed the ball back on top of the pile with the other balls, picked up a necklace, and put it around his neck.

As they walked outside, I asked if they were twins. They giggled and said, "No, just friends. We live down the road from each other."

Again I smiled and thought about the boy who lived down the road from me when I was little. We were inseparable on most days: riding our bikes, playing Wiffle ball, and trading baseball cards.

When they left, I realized how glad I was I'd answered the door. If I hadn't, I'd have missed the blessing that was standing on the other side. An opportunity missed if I would have pretended no one was home, something I've shamelessly done a time or two before.

What I loved most about this encounter was these kids both offered to give away toys to help other children in need. I didn't have to give them a long explanation why; they got it! Too many times as adults we put too much thinking into our giving. We question where our donation is going, how it is being used, and why. We hesitate to give because we are holding so tightly onto things of this world, whether they are material things or money. We should all strive to be childlike givers.

Giving Challenge

Next time your doorbell rings and you want to ignore it, answer it! There may be a blessing on the other side.

_____

_____

_____

_____

_____

Day 9: Dream Big

Written by: Emily Moulton

I remember sitting at the Versailles State Park for our first life coaching session. Stephanie asked me to participate in a "dream brainstorming" session—to write down anything and everything I dreamed of doing for my life. It was not easy or natural for me because I kept limiting it to what seemed plausible and realistic to actually happen. But Stephanie kept encouraging me to not limit the brainstorming to what felt realistic but to write down anything and everything I dreamed of doing. For example, she said, "Who would you like to meet?" and I said, "Condoleezza Rice," so we added that to the list.

When Stephanie surprised me for my birthday with the opportunity to hear Condoleezza Rice speak in person at the Columbia Club in Indianapolis, I was amazed! And so excited! It was a surreal and life-changing experience for me to hear Condoleezza Rice speak in person.

Condi said something in her speech that was life changing for me. She exhorted the audience to "pursue your passion" in regards to your career. In her life, she pursued her passion of studying Russian history, politics, and language while in college, even though she had no idea where that might lead her professionally. She pursued her passion. And as history unfolded during the 1980s, she was the right person at the right time that helped President George H. W. Bush end the cold war with the USSR. She applied everything she had studied about the USSR to impact history forever.

Ever since I heard Condi exhort us that day to "pursue your passion," I have done that in my professional life. At the time, I was disillusioned, confused, and in despair about where to go next in my career. The career I thought I would do for the rest of my life was causing me to be so miserable and stressed that I was getting physically sick. So I left the miserable job and was in between jobs when I heard Condi. Where was I to go next? Hearing Condi was the first step for me in the pursuit of my dream career. I started soul-searching and brainstorming my unique talents, abilities, and values in regards to work. Eventually, four years after hearing Condi, I moved into my dream career, which is to be a travel director and tour guide. I absolutely love my new profession. I am pursuing my passion and changing lives for the better in my own way. If Condi had not given me "permission" to pursue my passion professionally, I would probably still be in a dead-end job just to pay the bills.

The experience of seeing Condoleezza Rice in person taught me several things in addition to what I just stated about pursuing my passion. The experience taught me to dream big and not to limit my dreams to what seems realistic. It also taught me that "where there's a will, there's a way." Once the dream to meet Condoleezza Rice was on my to-do list, Steph showed me that dreams can come true if you have the will to pursue them. The final thing the experience taught me was the life-changing power of a friend who believes in me. My friend, Steph, gave me the gift of a life-changing experience. Her gift was a personal gift. She knew about my dream to meet Condoleezza Rice because she had invested so much time in knowing me and "dreaming big" with me. She used her talents and resources to give me a gift that altered the course of my life for the better. I am so thankful for my friend, Steph, who saw something I needed that I couldn't see in myself at the time. She taught me a life lesson about dreaming big through the gift of meeting Condoleezza Rice.

Giving Challenge

Sometimes the greatest thing we can do for others is to head up their cheering section. If you know your friends have dreams yet they don't believe in themselves to accomplish them, step up and help them out! Cheer for them! Encourage them! Let them know they always have your support. What is your dream? Write it down. Share it with a friend, and go after it!

_____

_____

_____

_____

_____

Day 10: Serendipity!

Serendipity is good fortune, luck, or the aptitude for making desirable discoveries by accident. It is also the title of one of my favorite chick flicks starring John Cusack and Kate Beckinsale. If you haven't seen it, check it out!

Sashaying through the doors of Pier One while admiring all the beautifully designed chairs, brightly colored pillows, and patterned dinnerware, I was on a mission to buy crackle stemware in a dazzling purple. I quickly located the glasses, picked up what I needed, and headed straight for the checkout. I had two gift cards burning a hole in my pocket and a couple of coupons. As I was checking out the cashier informed me, I could only use one of the coupons. Bummer!

In the line next to me was a couple and I handed them the unused coupon for 20 percent off. With the look of surprise in their eyes, the gentleman blurted out, "Serendipity!" This was not the reaction I anticipated. They thanked me for the coupon and my mission was accomplished. Their day had been made. The cashier was grinning ear to ear at this gesture of kindness that didn't cost me a dime.

Opportunities to show kindness are always presenting themselves to us. We can choose however we'd like to respond. In this case, I could have stuck the coupon back in my purse to use another day, but choosing to give it away felt so much better.

Giving Challenge

Seek out an opportunity to serendipitously surprise and bless another person today.

_____

_____

_____

_____

_____

Day 11: Miles and Memories

Airline miles. Every time we take a flight, we rack these babies up. In the past, I have converted accumulated miles into gift cards and magazines, but when I stumbled upon the option to donate miles to charity, it was a no-brainer, especially realizing I would lose the miles if I didn't use them. So why not donate them to a great cause?

Scrolling through the list, the Ronald McDonald House Charities immediately caught my attention. Suddenly, thoughts drifted back to my childhood. Memories fluttering around my mind of serving meals to families that were residing at the Ronald McDonald House of Indiana. Families whose children were fighting unimaginable battles with cancer and other life-threatening illnesses.

> The purpose of this life is not to be happy. It is to be useful, to be honorable, to the compassionate, to have it make a difference that you have lived and lived well.
>
> —Ralph Waldo Emerson

At the time I gave this gift, I didn't know a friend of mine would become a resident of the Ronald McDonald House of Indiana, as his child was diagnosed with a rare form of cancer and would need radiation and chemotherapy at a hospital away from home.

My friend was within driving distance of the hospital, so the airlines would not have benefitted him. It's interesting to stop and think about how a gift given today may help someone in the future. Maybe that is why you are being prompted to give.

Because of all the donations that are given to charities like the Ronald McDonald House, families like my friend's have one less thing to worry about when their child is going through the unimaginable.

I'm happy to report that my friend's son is doing amazing! At his six-month checkup, all of his scans were clear and his once bald head is covered with thick, brown hair. He finished a cross-country season, earned all A's, is back to full involvement with the youth group, and is a terrific drummer in the band.

Giving Challenge

Do you have excess airline miles you can donate? I encourage you to find an organization close to your heart and make this donation. Even a small amount makes a big difference!

_____

_____

_____

_____

_____

Day 12: Cotton Candy and the Pumpkin Show

The leaves are changing colors, the air is crisp, and carnival sounds and whiffs of elephant ears float through the air. In my hometown of Versailles, Indiana, it could only mean one thing: the Pumpkin Show has arrived. The Pumpkin Show is an annual tradition where local farmers grow pumpkins weighing over a thousand pounds, bands gather to march in the parade, friends from years past embrace with hugs, exchange life updates, and reminisce of the good old days.

My niece and nephew experiencing the magic of the Pumpkin Show ranks high on the list of the best things about being an aunt. Sharing memories with them of riding floats, twirling a baton, and marching in the band playing my trombone, I'm taken back to a time when life was simple and I didn't have a care in the world.

They're smart kids, they have learned that Aunt Stephie will treat them to almost anything at the Pumpkin Show. *Tickets for the rides? Of course! Someone to go on the rides with? Absolutely! No worries about my windblown hair! Want some cotton candy? Sure, you're going home with your parents!*

At times, I envied people who grew up in the big city, but at the Pumpkin Show, I'm reminded of how lucky I was to grow up in a small community. How I have the best group of friends a gal could ask for and that putting a smile on a child's face costs a couple of tickets, getting dizzy on the Sizzler, and a little cotton candy!

Giving Challenge

Do you have any family traditions? How can you share those experiences with the little ones in your life? If you don't have traditions, start one!

_____

_____

_____

_____

_____

Day 13: An American Hero

Old Glory flapping in the wind and the National Anthem booming through loud speakers cause puddles of tears to fill my eyes waiting for a blink to splash down my face. Images of friends that have served our country flash in mind.

I once asked my friend Rich why he served and he said, "The day I chose to serve was September 11, 2001. At the time, I was enrolled at the University of Evansville, studying criminal justice. I remember that day like it was yesterday, even the smell of the air outside as I sat on my porch thinking that everything from this point forward was going to change.

The next morning, I drove to the recruiter's office and joined the United States Navy. I often look back on that day, especially when people ask me why I did it. My response is simple. I love waking up every morning knowing that my sacrifice, and those of many others, made it possible for my loved ones and the people of this country to enjoy their freedom. Everything I am today is because of the sacrifices made and what I was taught in the service. I love that when I look at an American flag, I feel the most powerful swell of pride and love. I feel that I owe it to the people of the United States to ensure that everyone feels safer so that they can continue to cherish what this great country is all about: Life. Liberty. Freedom. The pursuit of happiness."

What did you feel on September 11? Was your first reaction to go serve our country? I know mine wasn't. I was scared. I wondered what was happening. I have often taken for granted my freedoms I have as an American.

Dan, a good friend, was getting ready to deploy to Iraq and a group of us gathered for his going-away party at a local restaurant. Walking into the doors of the restaurant, I was greeted by a consistent stream of friends. More than twenty people showed up to honor our friend. Prior to the party, I researched and found a list of items that were most needed by our soldiers in Iraq and put together a care package. I wanted him to know we were grateful for his service and we supported the job he was doing.

After the party was over, Dan came over to our house, sat on the couch, and talked about his job in the military, what he thought of the war, and politics. His insight and opinions gave me a lot to think about, and I was glad for this time to stay up and chat with him.

During Dan's deployment, I—and many others—prayed for his safety and the safety of all the men and women defending our freedom and fighting for the freedom of others. We are very lucky that Dan returned home safely from his deployment, but there were many that didn't return. Many that made the ultimate sacrifice. There are families who will live out the remainder of their days without their loved ones by their side. There are those that returned struggling with posttraumatic stress disorder, homelessness, and suicide. We must always remember the words inscribed on the Korean War Memorial in Washington, DC. "Freedom is not free."

Giving Challenge

Abundant opportunities exist to write letters to military servicemen and women serving overseas, to send care packages and thank-you notes, or to even offer a handshake and a thank-you for their service and sacrifice. Always be on the lookout for ways to make a difference.

_____

_____

_____

_____

_____

Day 14: Giving Away My Birthday Flowers

Spending my birthday on a business trip in Washington D.C, I was fortunate to be surrounded by great co-workers who did a fabulous job of making my day special. But my heart twinged with sadness as I wouldn't be spending the day with my hubby.

Working long hours and attending back-to-back meetings made for an exhausting day. Thoughts of my comfy bed danced in my head, but entering my room, I was distracted by an extravagant bouquet of flowers. The vase overflowed with roses, daisies, sunflowers, and lilies in an array of colors. My excitement couldn't be contained and there was no need to read the card, as I knew they were from my husband. The flowers meant so much to me because he thought to do something while I was away. He rarely gets me flowers, as he knows I think they are a waste of money, but today they were exactly what I needed. The perfect gift.

I spent the evening prepping my flowers for the journey home. The hotel staff joined in on the fun too, bringing me paper towels that I would drench in water the next morning, plastic baggies to transfer the flowers from the vase, and rubber bands to make sure the baggie was tightly around the stems. I was already envisioning where the flowers would sit on my desk and I would give the sunflowers to my sister, as they are her favorite flower.

If you want to draw attention to yourself at the airport, carry a large arrangement of flowers and you will receive countless stares. I wasn't even sure flowers could be taken through security, but guess what? They can! Placing the flowers on the conveyor belt, they were scanned and came through the other side intact. After making it through security, I was on a mission to locate a restroom. I approached an attendant at the information booth and asked for directions. The attendant, an older gentleman, pointed in the direction of the restroom and commented how beautiful my flowers were. I thanked him and headed on my way.

As I walked away, I heard a little voice in my head saying, give away the flowers.

What? I wasn't giving away *my* flowers. I loved them. I had spent time prepping them for travel and getting them through security, and I was taking them home!

The bathroom was surprisingly empty. I set the flowers on the ledge above the sink and prayed someone wouldn't steal them. When I came out to wash my hands, they were still there. Again, I heard a little voice say, give away the flowers.

Oh snap! I have always found it easy to give, but occasionally I felt challenged to give gifts I didn't want to give. This was definitely a gift that I did not want to give. My character was being tested. Was I only giving when it was convenient and easy, or was I giving from the heart and being selfless?

As I walked out of the restroom, I met my coworker who was talking to the gentleman at the information booth. As I approached, the gentleman again commented, "Those are such beautiful flowers; my wife would love them."

As he was uttering those words, I knew I was supposed to give my flowers to him. Stretching out my arm I said, "Here you go; take them!"

Chuckling, he said, "I was just complimenting you on the flowers; I don't want them."

I replied, "I know! Take these flowers and give them to your wife."

He was shocked and thrilled at the same time. He was getting ready to get off duty and said his wife would be so surprised.

My coworker was in disbelief as he watched me give away my birthday flowers. But my heart was smiling, knowing I had done the right thing. What an opportunity for a random act of kindness. I wish I could have been at that gentleman's home when he gave his wife those flowers. I wonder if he told her the story of what happened. I wondered if he paid it forward in some way and what difference this act of kindness made in his life, if any. I will never know, but that day, I learned to listen to that tug on my heart, as opportunities to be generous are all around if we look and listen. Would you give away your birthday flowers?

Several weeks after that day at the airport, my coworker called me excited. He shared how giving away my flowers had inspired him. He'd been in Home Depot that weekend, and after conversing with the cashiers, he left the store, went and bought them coffee, and returned to deliver it to them. The ladies to whom he gave the coffee, like the gentleman in the airport, were shocked and of course very grateful. No one had ever done something like that for them. His act of kindness is my goal of giving. To encourage others to give and to make a difference in the lives of people we know and to strangers, to create a ripple effect of giving that will change the world, one simple gift at a time.

Giving Challenge

Have you ever given a gift that was difficult for you to part with? What was it? I challenge you to listen for the small voice that might be nudging you to give something away cheerfully, especially when you'd rather keep it for yourself.

_____

_____

_____

_____

Day 15: Unexpected Friendship

Whenever my husband and I travel, we try something new and adventurous. It was the second day of our Mexican vacation and we had a Mayan Xtreme Adventure planned that included snorkeling in an underground cavern, zip-lining over the Mexican jungle, and rappelling off a seventy-foot tower. I awoke at 2:00 a.m. to the sound of pouring rain. I drifted back to sleep, and when my alarm went off four hours later, it was still raining cats and dogs. Debating as to whether or not we should cancel the trip, we knew if we didn't go on this day we might not get another chance.

When our guide, Carlos, arrived to pick us up, he said we could cancel, but he didn't think it would be raining where we were headed in Tulum because it was over an hour away and the weather was always different there than it was in Riviera Maya. We trusted his advice and piled into the van. We were a bit sleepy so we talked very little to Carlos on the way to our destination. Even though we didn't have much interaction with him prior to our excursion, he ended up being the best guide we have had on any vacation. He was knowledgeable, jovial, and always made us feel safe and comfortable, even right before he pushed me off the first tower for the zip-line!

We were in a great mood on the way back to the resort. The day was far better than we expected and snorkeling in the cave had topped my list of one of the most memorable moments in my life.

After spending the day with Carlos, I was interested in learning about his life. I told him how impressed I was with his English. Most of the staff we had encountered at the resort spoke broken English, but Carlos was fluent. He told us how when he started in the service industry, he would learn a word a day and was still continuing to learn. His philosophy on life, his country, and work ethic touched me greatly. It's rare to meet someone who is truly genuine with his nature, but Carlos certainly was. He loved his country and was saddened by what was happening on the northern border. He felt very strongly that what was happening was giving a black eye to all of his country. He loved Mexico, just like I love the United States of America.

Carlos gave me a new perspective on life. He was happy and lived a simple life. His day started at 4:30 a.m. and would end around 4:30 p.m. He worked six days a week for fifteen dollars per day. Let's just stop and think about that for a minute. Could you imagine working a twelve-hour day for only fifteen dollars? I couldn't. I could not comprehend how someone could live on fifteen dollars per day.

The more I talked with Carlos, the more I felt like I was talking with an old friend. I was sad for our trip to end. When we returned to our resort, it was again pouring rain. I noticed I didn't have enough cash for the amount of the tip I wanted to give Carlos. I gave him what I had and asked him to wait while I ran back to our room to grab more money. I ran all the way in the rain, and when I got back to the van, I was drenched. But I didn't care. Carlos hopped out of the van and I gave him the biggest tip I have given in my life. He tried to give me back what I had already given him and had a look of amazement in his eyes when I told him to keep that also. We stood in the rain hugging. My eyes started to well up with tears. I was sad to leave him, a friend I had only known for a day. He kissed me on the cheek. (This is a gesture many Mexicans do to greet or say good-bye to their friends.) I told him to have a blessed life and that I would be praying for him.

As I ran back to the room in the rain, tears of happiness streamed down my face. I can't explain the connection I had with Carlos. I think it is something that happens when we take time to treat each other as human beings, ask questions, and take a real interest in the lives of others. It is something I struggle with every day, but treating people as equals and not judging is something we should all strive for in our daily lives. We never know what others have been through, where they've come from, and what their aspirations are in life. Reach out to those you encounter; you just may make a difference in their lives, and they in yours.

After this life-changing experience, I submitted a review on Trip Advisor and made sure to specifically call out Carlos. Days later, I received a response from Carlos's employer that said, "Hola! Thank you for taking the time to share your experience. You have made Carlos's day with such an amazing review ... We cannot express how happy he felt when he read your comments."

I wonder what meant more to Carlos: the tip we gave him or the review and kind words. I have a sneaking suspicion the words meant more. Money is nice, but you never know when a kind word changes the course of someone's day.

Giving Challenge

Who might you encounter unexpectedly? When someone new enters your life, how can you bless them and take an interest in that person's life?

_____

_____

_____

_____

_____

Day 16: Letters in the Mail

Every once in a while, I'll receive a letter in the mail from a friend that completely makes my day. How often do we take time to handwrite a letter, put a stamp on an envelope, and drop it in a mailbox? We get so caught up in the ease and convenience of e-mails and text messages that written letters have fallen by the wayside of the past, even though they are often more meaningful and personal.

I try to make it a habit of sending one or more written notes to friends and family each week. The notes vary. Sometimes the cards are for a special occasion, other times it's for encouragement or to say thank you. The purpose doesn't matter. The fact you are taking the time to acknowledge a friend, family member or stranger and make them feel special is important. Cards are one of the cheapest gifts you can give but will make an immeasurable impact.

Giving Challenge

Take a few minutes today and write a letter of encouragement, a thank-you note, or just a hello. Let a friend know that you appreciate their friendship and support and thank them for being an active participant in your life. They will enjoy receiving a surprise in their mailbox.

_____

_____

_____

_____

Day 17: Experiencing Chicago

I love choosing Christmas gifts for my mom! One of my favorite gifts to give is experiences. Things are just that: things. And they usually end up on a shelf or stored in a closet, attached to no memory and enjoyed for a short time until they're forgotten. Experiences, however, create memories, and as I get older, the memories we make now are going to last a lifetime.

Growing up, I enjoyed listening to Chicago, but my mom loved that group! She couldn't get enough of the band members and their music. She'd listened to them for years and dreamed of seeing them live. As luck would have it, Chicago was in Indiana around Christmas and this would make the perfect gift. Logging into Ticketmaster the moment the tickets went on sale, I was ecstatic to secure fifth-row, center tickets.

Here's what my mom had to say about the night:

> "I love a two-for-one deal. That is what I received from Stephanie one year ago at Christmas. The group Chicago is my all-time favorite. As an early gift, she surprised me with two tickets. I asked her who was going with me. She said, "Me!" It is still one of my favorite evenings. We had a blast singing, dancing, and laughing together. I think I smiled through the whole concert. Our seats were fabulous. I was so close I could see the sweat dripping from the band

members' foreheads and the expressions on their faces. What a fun night!"

As I looked around, I'm pretty sure I was the youngest female in the crowd. Most were women in their fifties to seventies, swooning over the men in the band.

I could have bought my mom a sweater or a purse, but the experience of seeing a live show together created a memory we'd share forever. I wouldn't have it any other way.

Giving Challenge

The next time you need to buy a gift, think about giving an experience instead of a thing. Concert or play tickets are big hits for adults, and zoo and children's museum passes are popular with children. What experience would you like to give to someone you love?

_____

_____

_____

_____

_____

Day 18: Pencils and Prayers

Are you a collector of Dishes? Dolls? Figurines? Shoes? Purses? Growing up, I didn't have a huge interest in toys. I was allergic to stuffed animals, and being surrounded mostly by boys, I played sports, school, and created adventures in the woods near my home. Even though I didn't enjoy toys, I loved collecting stickers, postcards from around the world, and pencils.

Pencils? you might be thinking. I know I'm a nerd. And when I say "collecting," I mean it in the true sense of the world. I treasured these little wooden sticks. I didn't sharpen them, didn't use them for homework, and stored them safely in a school box. Pulling the pencils out of their box on occasion to admire the intricate details, visualizing where the pencil came from, and then I'd neatly pack them back in the box. This box traveled with me to every dorm room, apartment, and house I've ever lived in. I've been hauling these pencils around with me for over thirty years!

Since childhood, I've collected close to 150 pencils, none of which are yellow, standard No. 2 pencils. They were all different colors with various sayings etched in the wood. Some of my favorites came from museums in Chicago and Washington, DC.

My pencil collection made a final move in May 2011, when the town of Joplin, Missouri, was flattened and destroyed by an F5 tornado. A total of 158 people lost their lives in the destruction. The citizens of this community were in desperate need of basic necessities and clothing. I had just cleaned out my closet and didn't have any clothes to give away, so I took money from my giving budget to buy toiletries. I purchased things like washcloths, toothpaste, toothbrushes, toilet paper, contact cases, soap, and ponchos. School supplies were also needed, so I opened my office closet, which was packed with supplies. I pulled out pens, paper, and folders. As I was going through my supplies, my box of pencils caught my eye. I thought, *Oh no, God! Not my pencils!*

One thing I've learned through my giving journey is that when God speaks, I need to listen. I firmly believe ideas don't randomly pop in my head, especially when it comes to giving. Like I said, I'd been hauling these pencils around for years. I've donated school supplies to the local school every year; I purchase supplies for children I know, and not one time in my life has the thought crossed my mind to give my pencil collection away.

Until this fateful day.

Even though I knew what needed to be done, it was hard for me to part with my special collection. Sometimes God doesn't make giving simple and easy. Sometimes it is a sacrifice. And although these were just pencils, they were tied to many memories. They came home with me from vacations, were given to me from friends, and came from places I've worked, in a way documenting my life.

Sitting crossed-legged on the floor and sorting pencils, I had a calming peace come over me as I realized a child who just lost everything might, for a moment, find joy in a cool pencil. A brightly colored pencil with sparkles and glitter, Bible verses, and other words of encouragement.

After I gave away my pencils, I questioned if collections were meant to be kept and at the perfect time be given away. I often wonder about my pencil collection. It's been several years since I gave them away. I wonder about the children that received them and how their lives were forever changed by something so destructive. I also think how beautiful it was to see thousands of people, strangers, from across the country coming together to help a community in need. Did the acts of kindness somehow change their lives for the better? Was someone who was lacking in faith led to Christ? Did people who were lonely become surrounded by people who were all in the same boat struggling to rebuild and develop an unexpected friendship? I don't know. But maybe through it all, there is still a pencil in a drawer or a pocket that was sent all the way from Indiana to Missouri in hopes of making a difference.

Giving Challenge

Do you have a special collection that can be given to someone suffering through a difficult time? If so, consider giving it away! What a blessing it will be to someone else in great need.

_____

_____

_____

_____

_____

Day 19: The Guardian Bell

I can remember the day my husband and his friend traveled to Chicago to pick up his friend's motorcycle. When my husband returned, he told me he'd bought his friend a Guardian Bell for his bike. I'd never heard of a Guardian Bell. Have you? I did a little research and found there is a legend about this little bell: bikers hang the bell on their motorcycles and it keeps the riders from bad luck while traveling. The legend also describes how the rider will have better luck if the Guardian Bell is received as a gift from someone rather than if the rider purchases it for himself or herself.

Are you a believer in legends? I'm not a believer in legends, but I am a believer in thoughtful gifts. I thought the bells were cute and my husband would probably enjoy having one on his bike. One evening, I searched through tons of Guardian Bell designs and settled on one that was simple but perfect for Mike. It was a pewter bell displaying the American flag to symbolize his service to the Indiana State Police and to represent his friend, Scott, who died in the line of duty.

Late one night while my husband was still at work, I wrote and left a note at the top of the stairs along with the Guardian Bell, knowing Mike would find it when he returned home from his shift. The note read,

> My gift to you today. I ordered this bell because I wanted you to always have a piece of me with you when you are

riding. The flag is to honor Scott, as I know he would want to be riding with you. Thank you for being so good to me, even when I don't deserve it. Love always.

I must admit that even though I don't believe this Guardian Bell brings good luck, I do know my husband's friend had his bike painted, forgot to put the bell back on his bike, and had a minor crash while they were out riding. My husband teased his friend that the accident wouldn't have happened if he'd had his Guardian Bell!

Giving Challenge

Are you ever shopping and see something you think a friend would like but dismiss the thought and don't purchase the gift? Next time, buy it! If it's affordable and you think it'll make a friend's day, then just do it. These are some of the best gifts!

_____

_____

_____

_____

_____

Day 20: Scouting for Food

Tucked through the handle of my front door was a note from the local Boy Scout troop letting me know they would be collecting nonperishable items for their annual food drive. Not wanting to forget to pick up items, I placed the note on my desk as a reminder. However, the busyness of the week got the best of me and the reminder became buried on my office desk. Has this ever happened to you?

The day of the Boy Scout food drive, I was cleaning off my desk and sorting through paperwork when I came across the note. Crap! I had ten minutes before the Boy Scouts showed up on my porch to collect donations. Shooting straight up of my chair, I hurried down the stairs to the pantry to examine what food I had in stock to give.

As it turned out, I had plenty canned and boxed goods to fill several bags. As I was carrying the bags to the front door, I paused in gratitude, realizing how immensely blessed I was to have a pantry full of food. In a moment's notice, I was able to stock several bags up with food—food I take for granted.

This journey taught me to be thankful for the necessities in life and to notice that many are not as lucky as I am. I'm more cognizant that others struggle on a daily basis. We always need to be thinking, *How can I ease someone's struggle today?*

I love the idea of a food drive because even though my couple of bags may not go far, and only feed a family for several days. The compound effect of everyone in the community donating food makes a tremendous impact. Never underestimate the power of a small gift.

Giving Challenge

Support your local food pantry by collecting and dropping off a couple of items. When shopping, add an extra can or two to be donated.

_____

_____

_____

_____

_____

Day 21: The Right Stuff

Were you a child of the 1980s and 1990s? I was born in the late 1970s, which put me right on track to become a crazy fan of New Kids on the Block. I was in middle school when they stormed onto the music scene, and they have been a part of my life ever since.

I remember those days well: my walls plastered with pictures of NKOTB, especially Jonathan, my favorite band member. I had buttons the size of my head, puzzles, cups, T-shirts, and even a pillowcase! Every time I joined my mother on a trip to the grocery store, I headed straight to the magazine rack to check out the latest teen heartthrob magazines. I'd purchase a copy or two so I would have new pictures for my wall. *Obsessed* is putting it lightly. Who was your teen idol growing up?

I remember the day like it was yesterday. NKOTB announced a tour stop in Cincinnati, Ohio. My sister and a couple of our friends were *dying* to see them in concert. This was years before the Internet, Smartphones, and apps, so getting tickets were not as convenient as it is today. I set my alarm early that day, as oversleeping would have been disastrous. Entering the number in the phone, I was ready to hit talk the moment the clock ticked to 10:00 a.m. I wiggled my fingers in preparation of hitting redial after redial. The moment came and, as expected, a busy signal. As fast as my fingers would move, I hit redial, and yet again a busy signal. This went on several more times. Between the redial and busy signal, I started to pray, "Dear Lord, please let us get tickets. Amen!"

Then it happened: no busy signal. A lady's voice echoed through the phone and I danced around like a teenage girl. My biggest dream, at the time, had come true. My sister and I were going to see New Kids on the Block!

We spent what seemed like hours getting all dolled up for the concert, in hopes of a chance encounter with Jonathan and Danny, our favorites! No such luck, but that evening is still one of my favorite childhood moments.

Fast-forward to 2011. New Kids on the Block was reuniting and touring along with the Backstreet Boys. I enjoyed the Backstreet Boys and their music brought back memories of my junior year in college when my roommate and I would put in a *Seven Minute Abs* VHS tape, crank up their music, and work out to their jams. My roommate's boyfriend made a ton of fun of us, but we loved it and giggled the entire time.

So when I heard that NKOTB and the Backstreet Boys were coming to Indianapolis, I called my sister to see if she wanted to go to the concert. Of course she couldn't resist a night of hot guys, good music, rekindling childhood memories, and a night out with her big sis. We agreed on what we wanted to pay for the tickets, but I decided to surprise her with upgraded tickets. Instead of sitting in the nosebleeds, I purchased seats in the lower level. She didn't realize what was happening until we started walking in and I led her down instead of up. Our seats were incredible! As soon as the lights went down, my sister and I were taken back to all those years ago. Like at our first concert, we stood the entire time and screamed like high school girls.

It's been five years since that night and we still love to talk about how much fun we had. Quality time and making memories with friends and families is one of the best gifts you can ever give. The time each chooses to intentionally invest with others doesn't have to be as extravagant as tickets to a show. Entertaining people in your home, cooking a meal, going for a walk in the park, or sitting on the couch together and catching up on life are all an investment in the lives of those you love. All of these are equally important gifts and are wonderful to give to others and yourself. It's moments like these when I find myself quoting the movie *Hope Floats*. "My cup runneth over."

Giving Challenge

In what ways do you surprise your family? Think of a way you could surprise a family member during your own forty-day challenge. Maybe it's scheduling a day at the park, taking them to their favorite museum, surprising them with their favorite specialty coffee, and shooting the breeze. Whatever it is, just take time to invest in others.

_____

_____

_____

_____

_____

Day 22: Pamper Night

According to the National Coalition on Domestic Violence, on average, nearly twenty people per minute are physically abused by an intimate partner in the United States. One in fifteen children is exposed to intimate partner violence each year, and 90 percent of these children are eyewitnesses to this violence. Victims of intimate partner violence lose a combined total of eight million days of paid work each year and the cost of intimate partner violence exceeds $8 billion per year.

These crimes not only affect the victims but also their children, family, places of employment, schools, and communities. Domestic violence causes a ripple effect to everyone and everything connected to the victim.

We, like many communities throughout the United States, are fortunate to have a domestic violence shelter to assist men, women, and children fleeing from scary and dangerous situations. Our local shelter is the The Caring Place, and through Facebook, I found out a local church was hosting a Pamper Night for the women of the shelter.

Pamper Night is an incredible evening where, once the women and children enter the doors of the church, they are not to lift a finger. The volunteers take care of and love on them, show them kindness, and give them the respect they deserve. They are served a meal, including tons of desserts at their fingertips the entire evening, and receive massages, pedicures, manicures, haircuts and styles, makeup, goody baskets, clothing, and lots of hugs.

I contacted the organizer of the event to see what they needed or how I could help. I really wanted to volunteer for the event, but the day conflicted with vacation so a donation was going to have to suffice. I chose to give marshmallows and pretzels that would be used for the women to dip in chocolate, a treat I knew the women were sure to love. The church was also collecting travel-sized items to put in baskets for their guests. This was great! I travel a lot and always hoard the shampoo, conditioner, and lotion from hotels. I had the items stocked in my linen closet and this was my chance to put them to good use. I was able to donate fifteen bottles of each item.

Over the years, I have gotten to know the organizer of the event, Jeni, and I was curious of its beginning. And her answer shocked me. She shared with me that the youth group in her church was asked two simple questions. Who in the community needs us and Jesus and how can we help them?

I couldn't believe this event had started with questions posed to youth. Children often amaze me in their compassion and generosity toward others. Jeni also shared with me the following: "I grew up in an abusive home. I knew the fear, pain, loneliness, and insecurities. I wanted to ease that for them, even for just a moment. To feel the love and acceptance of people and Christ."

Wow! Jeni took a terribly tragic event in her childhood and turned it into a life-changing night for women in our community. Since 2011, I have had the opportunity to volunteer at Pamper Night and what I witnessed was nothing short of a miracle.

Stepping through the threshold of the church doors, slouching shoulders and lacking eye contact, few words were spoken and little to no physical contact was made. Greeting the women one by one, the volunteers were full of acceptance, love, and smiles. After several hours of nothing but undivided attention and love, a transformation takes place. Preparing to leave the event, there are lots of hugs, tears, laughter, and chatter bellowing throughout the room. Heads and shoulders are held high, eye contact is made, and lives are changed in a matter of hours, all because the youth of a church had an idea to pamper women who were not victims but survivors.

Giving Challenge

According to the CDC, NIJ, and DOJ, one of every four women will be a victim of domestic violence. There are women in your community that need help. Lend a helping hand when given the opportunity or reach out to your local domestic violence shelter and inquire on their current needs. If you collect toiletries from hotels, I challenge you to donate these items to nonprofits in your area. Of course I'm not encouraging you to steal from the housekeeping cart; take what is sitting on the counter that you didn't use. I have found homeless and domestic violence shelters can always use these types of items. Looking for an even bigger challenge? Locate your local domestic violence shelter, gather a few women from your community, and plan your own Pamper Night!

_____

_____

_____

_____

_____

Day 23: A Smile for a Stranger

I'm a bit embarrassed by this gift. Not at the gift itself but that I don't give it away more often. As my husband and I were pulling into Costco, we noticed a man standing at the entrance to the parking lot. His beard was scruffy, clothes tattered, and he held a sign I couldn't read. I commented to my husband that I had seen him there before—and that was the extent of our conversation.

By the time we parked our car, found a cart, browsed the aisles permeated with items we didn't need, and filled our cart with the things we did, the man at the side of the road slipped from my mind.

I won't say he's homeless because I'm not sure of his situation. He may have a home but needed money for food. He may not even need money but is still trying to collect it from those passing by. I don't know his story, and does it really matter? Should his story influence whether we give or not? This is a hard lesson to learn, and one I still struggle with, but I'm trying.

We paid for our groceries and loaded up our car, and as we started to pull out, I saw the man still standing on the roadside while holding his sign. I had a few seconds to decide how I would respond.

I'm embarrassed to admit this, but other times in a similar situation I would have looked the other way. Maybe you would too. We justify it by thinking if we don't look, we won't see the person in need. On this particular day, I knew I could once again turn away, but I couldn't do it.

As we approached him, I looked the man in his eyes, nodded, and gave a simple smile and a slight raise of my hand. I acknowledged him. And you know what happened? He smiled back and waved. We had made a connection. My eyes filling with tears, I realized maybe money wasn't his need after all.

Giving Challenge

Put yourself in the position of the person the side of the road, sometimes with their families, holding signs, and reaching out for help. Next time you encounter someone in need, how will you respond?

_____

_____

_____

_____

_____

Day 24: Giving Hearts a Hand

Many people sit on the sidelines complaining about issues in our world and have ideas of what needs to be done, but few take action. As a high school sophomore, my now brother-in-law, Doug, was diagnosed with hypertrophic cardiomyopathy, a heart condition that causes stress on the heart due to thickening of the tissue of the heart muscle. Under the watchful eye of some fantastic medical professionals, Doug has led a normal, active life through medication and close observation of the condition. But many teenagers, in particular student athletes, are not so lucky. You've heard the stories in the news of a "healthy" kid playing basketball and dropping dead on the court. My brother-in-law was one of the lucky ones that caught his condition in time before tragedy could occur.

Over the years, he saw a gap in the physical screenings for student athletes. A gap that his organization, Giving Hearts a Hand (www.givingheartsahand.org), now fills. GHH mission is to "inform local communities about heart conditions in young athletes, while funding cardiac screenings that will create awareness and potentially save lives." He and my sister, who run the organization, hope to help prevent tragic situations from occurring in young athletes through raising awareness of symptoms and treatments of undetected heart conditions, as many sudden cardiac arrest events happen during a sporting event or practice.

The year I started my giving journey, my sister and brother-in-law started on their own giving journey and founded Giving Hearts a Hand. They decided to no longer sit on the sideline wishing someone would help save the lives of young athletes succumbing to sudden cardiac arrest. Having a personal connection with heart disease and love of sports, Doug felt led to make a difference in young athletes' lives. Since 2011, GHH has screened hundreds of student-athletes and potentially saved lives. Below is an e-mail from a mother whose son was screened.

> My name is x, and I have 2 sons who play soccer at Center Grove High School. Thanks to you guys and IU, you saved my freshman son's life. He had the Echos for Athletes screening just over a week ago and they found about a 3 cm hole in the septum of his upper chambers of his heart. Needless to say we are shocked, and it has changed our lives. We were not aware of any symptoms or problem. He was a healthy 15-year-old boy, as far as we knew. We have had another Echo done and talked to a cardiologist who has referred us to a Riley cardiologist. Until we talk to Dr. Hoyer, we are not 100% sure what will be done, but we believe a heart catheterization will fix it. If not, then open heart. My family and I are so very grateful for you funding and setting this up. I am advocating to everyone I know to get this done! So blessed and forever thankful.

If you see a need in your community and you have a constant tug on your heart to take action, *do!* You never know. You may just save a life!

Giving Challenge

If you have a child, get their heart screened. If you don't have a child, share this story with a friend with children and encourage them to get their children's hearts screened.

_____

_____

_____

_____

_____

Day 25: Twenty-Five Years of Sobriety

Dining out at my favorite restaurant in Indianapolis, I excused myself from the table and searched for the ladies' room. Our server happened to be nearby and showed me the way. We had made a connection earlier as she apologized for carding our table. Making light of the situation and joking it was flattering to be carded, I assured her there was no reason to apologize. I explained that I was a former Excise police officer and understood she was simply following the law.

Walking to the restroom, she asked, "As a former officer, do you have any advice for me?" I answered, "Always be responsible. When in doubt, card and never over serve. Remember if you over serve someone and they get behind the wheel of the car and kill someone, some of the responsibility comes back to you. You don't want that on your conscience."

Looking at me intently, she said, "Tomorrow I will be twenty-five years sober. I used to be that drunk driver. I could have killed someone. I carry my coin in my pocket right next to my wine opener."

Without thinking, I asked, "May I give you a hug?" Embracing, it was if I could feel the weight she carried float away. We continued chatting and I was moved she would open up to me—a stranger—about something so personal. Leaving, I gave her another hug and said, "By the way, I'm Stephanie."

Processing these gifts is difficult. At times it's overwhelming to imagine what another person has been through and why I was put in their path. Maybe she needed those hugs, encouragement, or a safe place to share her story; I don't know. Engage with people. Give them your time, and be open to question. Offer advice if asked, and if appropriate, give a hug. I can guarantee the impact you make will be nothing compared to the blessings you will receive.

Giving Challenge

Have you met a stranger whom you've been able to encourage and support through conversation? I challenge you to chat with someone new whose path you cross today. Fill that person with encouraging words, and receive the blessing of blessing others!

_____

_____

_____

_____

_____

Day 26: Donuts and Garage Doors

Mammograms. My friend says, "Mammograms are like getting your boobs smashed in the garage door!" And I think she is right, though I don't want to test her theory.

Arriving for my annual encounter with the "garage door," I signed in and anxiously waited to be called back. Thoughts passed through my mind as this was a stressful day for most women. A day that can change the course of your life. Like me, I'm sure you know someone that has unfortunately lost her battle to breast cancer.

"Stephanie!" exclaimed the nurse. As I was following her to the changing room, an emergency occurred and I was left to wait ... again. Continuing to wait, the nurse popped in periodically, ensuring I was okay. She was a servant getting me water and magazine and spending time getting to know me. Unlike other appointments, I wasn't stuck in a room wondering what was going on. I felt special and a priority and it made all the difference in my day.

Several days later, I wrote a thank-you note to the nurse and picked up a box of Munchkins from Dunkin Donuts. It was a small token of my appreciation for the kindness she showed me. After swinging by the hospital to pick up paperwork, I left the treat with the receptionist and went on my merry way. I'd like to think this gift was the pick-me-up she needed to get her through the day and that the donuts were shared with coworkers as her way of paying it forward.

Giving Challenge

Send an e-mail or mail a card to someone who has shown you compassion. This could be something from last week, month, or year. No matter the length of time passed, the acknowledgment of their kindness will warm their heart.

_____

_____

_____

_____

_____

Day 27: The Least of These

Have you ever stopped to think about how blessed you are to have a home? The churches in our community rotate housing homeless men during the winter months. It's a collaborative effort relying on people to donate time and meals. It's 4:15 a.m. I roll out of bed, stumble to the closet, and put on the first outfit that catches my eye. Jogging down the stairs and out the door, I hop in my car, and as I'm pulling out of the garage, I notice the darkness and no stirring from my neighbors. Fifteen minutes later, I swing through McDonald's to pick up a hot breakfast in hopes of warming and filling the men's bellies for the day ahead. Volunteers greet me at the door and are more than willing to take the food off my hands.

When I return home, breakfast is on my mind. I open the refrigerator and there sat several gallons of milk I was supposed to take to the church. What was I going to do with all this milk? As the thought flitted out of mind, I had my answer. My neighbor has three growing boys and I'm sure she'd appreciate the gift. Waiting several hours to make sure they were awake, I hauled the milk across the street. My neighbor graciously accepted the milk and assured me it would be consumed by week's end.

Jogging back across the road, my breath was taken away by the bone-chilling air. I could hardly tolerate being out for even a minute; I couldn't imagine getting through the day exposed to this weather. I was overpowered by the thought of not having a warm place to sleep and grateful we have churches opening their doors to bring warmth to others. I am lucky to live in a community that saw a need and filled a gap for homeless men.

Every time I see a homeless person, I try not to judge. I don't know their story and what led them to their circumstances. And usually Matthew 25:33–40 comes to mind.

> On the last day, Jesus will say to those on His right hand, "Come, enter the Kingdom. For I was hungry and you gave me food, I was thirsty and you gave me drink, I was sick and you visited me." Then Jesus will turn to those on His left hand and say, "Depart from me because I was hungry and you did not feed me, I was thirsty and you did not give me to drink, I was sick and you did not visit me." They will ask Him, "When did we see You hungry, or thirsty or sick and did not come to Your help?" And Jesus will answer them, "Whatever you neglected to do unto one of these least of these, you neglected to do unto Me."

Giving Challenge

Find an opportunity to give to the homeless in your own community.

_____

_____

_____

_____

_____

Day 28: The Giving Jar

Growing up, my parents taught my sister and me lots of valuable lessons. Work ethic, hustle, doing more than expected, doing things right the first time, and material things aren't as important as experiences and traditions. But the most important thing my parents taught us was about giving to others. This journey, even though motivated by reading a book, would not have happened if my parents hadn't instilled a giving spirit in me as a child. It is my hope that if you weren't taught this as a child, this book will in some ways help you grow the giving spirit that I know is inside of you.

My niece Josie, now ten, is the light of my world. My husband and I don't have children but I'm sure if we had a girl, she'd be like Josie; I often refer to her as my mini me because we have a bond that melts my heart. My sister and brother-in-law have done a terrific job equipping her with a giving spirit, just as my parents did for us. When Josie was five years old, my sister and brother-in-law gave her a giving jar.

The giving jar is a little jar used to collect money to spend on gifts for others. My niece has always been taught to divide any money she receives and put a portion into her giving jar. One day I decided to donate to her giving jar. I want to encourage her to give and let her know I support her giving projects. I am proud of her for saving money to give away to others.

Giving Challenge

Do you have a giving jar? Whose life could you bless and increase through this means of saving and giving? Think of a child in your life and give them a giving jar with a couple of dollars to jump-start their giving journey.

Day 29: Between Me and You

It's interesting how God puts people in my path I need to meet. In this case, it was Winston, the author of the Between Me and You journals. I met Winston at a conference and several days later sent him an email inviting him to breakfast. I was intrigued by his company and wanted to learn more. He graciously accepted, and we have been supporting our business adventures ever since. Here is a sneak peak on how one of his journals impacted my life.

On Mother's Day, my sister and I gave my mom the *Between Me and You—Mom* journal. It is a way for my mom to document our lives together and a keepsake I will treasure long after she is gone.

After my mom completed the journal, she returned the respective copies to my sister and me. Snuggling up in my favorite chair, I read the journal cover to cover. It was *amazing!* I learned things about my mom I never knew, things about her and my dad, her family, and her dreams for the future. I learned about the sadness and joy surrounding my birth that I hadn't known about until reading the journal. My mom wrote,

> The day we brought you home was filled with people coming and going all day and evening long. I was there all day except for leaving to go out to the farm to see Grandma Braley. Grandpa passed away that afternoon. A friend from Tangelwood Church wrote in a card that read, "You were the rosebud and he was the rose that withered."

I learned more about her dreams for me and regrets she had in her life, and she gave me a ton of great advice through her favorite quotes. My favorite quote she included was by Joyce Meyer.

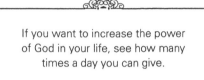

If you want to increase the power of God in your life, see how many times a day you can give.

—Joyce Meyer

Wow. Now that is a quote to ponder and then put into action. I think it's a perfect fit for *The Giving Challenge*. Our mission in life should be to lift each other up, not tear one another down, to show the love of Christ through our actions, and to be an angel to those in need.

After reading through the journal, I texted my sister to see if she had read her journal. She hadn't. She'd stuck it in a drawer and forgotten about it. Here's a bit of our text conversation:

Me: Have u read your journal from mom?

Cortney: No. Why? Is it good? I figured I would cry so I haven't yet!

Me: It's good … And yes, I cried!

Cortney: I figured … I may start reading it tonight then.

(Later that day …)

Cortney: Love that Nanna [our grandma] was awarded the "spirit stick!"

Me: I know, right?

Cortney: I just laughed out loud that Mom and Dad double-dated with Owen and Hope. These books are great! I need to get one to fill out for Josie while I can still remember stuff ... Ha! ☺

Me: I know. U can order them off Amazon.

On our first breakfast together I picked up the tab. It was a "thank-you" for accepting a request to meet with a stranger. I love that five years ago we were strangers and now I call him friend.

Giving Challenge

Who has given you a life-changing gift? What difference did it make in your life? How can you give back and thank them?

_____

_____

_____

_____

_____

Day 30: A Visit to the Past

As a blogger, I know the importance of readership. I try to support my blogging friends by reading and encouraging them throughout the process. Blogging is a big commitment, and most of us bloggers write because we believe our words can have great impact on the lives of our readers, not merely for personal satisfaction.

Kyle, my dear friend since kindergarten, wrote an amazing blog. He is extremely creative and wrote with the history buff in mind. His work truly is a must read. Here is an excerpt:

> This site is dedicated to my grandfathers and their experiences before, during, and after World War II. Philip Leland Givan, 2nd Battalion, 24th Marines, 4th Division Fleet Marine Force—the Pacific Theater of World War II. Robert Eugene Parker, 530th Field Artillery Battalion, 5th Army, 5th Division, United States Army—the European Theater of World War II. Initially, this site will follow my journey of tracing the history of several Japanese items my grandfather brought home from the Pacific. I hope to track down the families of the men who carried these items into battle. Ultimately, they ended up in a cardboard box in my grandfather's closet until the year 2000, when I began my senior honors thesis at Ball State University. Over time, I hope to expand this site to include stories of the veterans

who served with my grandfathers, photos, memories, and links to other resources and sites.

On this particular day, I took the time to read through his blog, appreciate his photographs, promote his blog on my Facebook page, and write him a note of encouragement. I believe the work he has done has affected many lives and brought joy to many families. Kyle is definitely an example of a single person making a significant difference.

Giving Challenge

Today I challenge you to support my friend Kyle by taking the time to read his blog and leave a comment letting him know your thoughts. You can find his blog at http://awakeningthepast-wwii. blogspot.com/. If you don't want to read his blog, find a blog that interests you, comment, and share on social media.

_____

_____

_____

_____

_____

Day 31: Coffee Shop, a Painting, and the Bible

Exiting the local coffee shop, Uptown Café, I noticed a couple of beautiful paintings on the wall. I was drawn, no pun intended, to one painting in particular. I loved it, but I knew the colors— purples and blues—didn't match anything in my house. Instead I envisioned a similar painting with colors of reds, oranges, and yellows to coordinate and hang in my office. I had to have the artist's information so I turned around, asked the barista, and she provided me with an e-mail address.

I e-mailed the artist, Michelle Pendergrass, and several weeks later, she was in my home, viewing my office colors so she could create a commissioned piece of art for me. Immediately connecting, I knew God had brought her into my life for a reason. She had great energy and positivity, was motivated, and shared with me the story of how she started painting. I love meeting people who are explorers in life and with their careers. It is rare for people to follow their passions and do what they truly love on a daily basis.

This is the second time on this journey when I have encountered a stranger, sent a random e-mail about their product, and developed a friendship. I think life is full of opportunities to do great things and meet amazing people, but we must stop long enough to listen to that little voice telling us to make that call or send that e-mail. It is the same voice that tells me to call an old friend, flash a smile, or help a stranger. Throughout this journey, I have tried to focus on listening, helping others, and giving of myself. Most days we will never know the impact of one small action.

Michelle had mentioned she could always use more Bibles, as she weaves Bible clippings into her paintings. I took note of what she said and on this day I gave a Bible to my new friend. Want to see the amazing artwork I saw in Uptown Café? Check out Michelle's website at www.michellependergrass.com.

Giving Challenge

Whose dream can you support? An artist, an author, or anyone who makes a living from their creativity? Your patronage and support will be greatly appreciated!

_____

_____

_____

_____

_____

Day 32: What Can You Do for Brown?

The UPS truck beeped as it backed into our driveway. Without thinking about it, I grabbed an unopened box of South Bend Chocolates from my office, raced down the stairs, and opened the front door before the UPS man could ring the doorbell. Greeting him with the chocolates, he seemed a bit confused, then surprised and grateful. I told him I was thankful for the job he does. He must have thanked me about five times before walking back to his truck. I had a feeling this random act of kindness made his day.

In the book *29 Gifts*, author Cami Walker not only journals about what she gave but what she received. I think it's important to take notice of the gifts we receive on a daily basis, and whether big or small, we need to show gratitude. This same morning, I was given that very opportunity.

As the UPS truck drove away, I walked to the mailbox, and waiting there for me was a medium-sized manila envelope. I opened it up and found a homemade card from my four-year-old (now ten) niece, Josie. On the front, she had written my name, and on the inside, she'd put a dolphin sticker with a drawing of the two of us holding hands. My sister included a note.

> "Jos go these animal stickers in her stocking for Christmas and the other day I went up to her room and the dolphin was the only one left on the sheet. I asked her what she was doing with the dolphin and she said, "Saving it for Stephie!"

Children listen; they learn. They can be taught giving at a very early age, and they will put what they learned into action immediately. My office is filled with pictures colored by my niece, nephew, and godson. Why? Because they are little givers and I want to encourage them to continue to give! It never ceases to amaze me how giving children are, and teaching them the joy of giving from an early age is invaluable. Are you raising a giver?

Giving Challenge

If you have children, I encourage you to teach them about giving. Giving is learned. Who knows? Maybe twenty years from now they will be writing about their giving journey!

_____

_____

_____

_____

_____

Day 33: Shoes Serving a Purpose

One of the top ten New Year's resolutions is to get—and stay—organized. If I had to bet, I would guess you had this on your list of resolutions or things to accomplish in the New Year. Have you taken steps to meet this New Year's resolution? If not, maybe Soles4Souls will motivate you to get organizing and make a difference at the same time. Soles4Souls is a nonprofit global social enterprise committed to fighting poverty through the collection and distribution of shoes and clothing.

Taking five minutes and shuffling through my closet, I quickly gathered five pairs of shoes to donate. I originally chose only two pairs, until I asked myself, "Really, Stephanie? Really? You probably have forty pairs of shoes and you can't find five to donate?" After this self-talk, I quickly picked out three more pairs to give away. Guilt and the knowledge of how blessed I am will get me every time.

Giving Challenge

Take five to ten minutes to go through your closet, and then choose one or more pairs of shoes to donate to Soles4Souls. If you don't have shoes to donate, post a message on Facebook that you are collecting shoes. And when you receive five or ten pairs, mail them in. To learn more about Soles4Souls and how to donate new or used shoes, go to http://www.soles4souls.org.

_____

_____

_____

_____

_____

Day 34: The ROI of Giving™

I love celebrating holidays. I mean, nowadays there is a holiday for everything. You love peanut butter? There is a peanut butter lover's day. You like your sibling? There is sibling's day. The list goes on and on. But there are days and even weeks that are dedicated to the brave men and women that serve our country. According to www.nleomf. org, in 1962, President Kennedy declared May 15 as National Peace Officers Memorial Day, and the calendar week in which the date falls is National Police Week.

Sitting in the local Subway, munching on chips, I looked up and saw two police officers in line. While the sandwich artist was putting the final touches on the officers' sandwiches I hopped up from my seat, told the cashier I wanted to pay for their meals, and handed him my credit card. The officers didn't notice at the time what I was doing and I didn't say, "Hey, I paid for your lunch!" I just quietly walked back to my seat.

Moments later, one of the officers came over, extended his hand, and said, "Thanks so much for lunch. You didn't have to do that, but I appreciate it."

I shook his hand and said, "Well it's National Police Week and I wanted to thank you for the job you do."

As I was getting ready to sit back down, the other officer came over and we had the same conversation. I was glad I could do something to show these two officers that there are people in the community who support the job they do.

As I was leaving, I looked down at my receipt and noticed Subway had given me 50 percent off the officer's meals, which I believe is something they regularly do for those in uniform. A bonus gift!

The following day, I was at a coffee shop with friends. They were already sitting down as I was waiting to order my hot chocolate. Just as I was getting ready to pay, one of my friends hopped up and paid for my drink. It was definitely an unexpected surprise. I immediately chuckled and thought, *That's the ROI (Return on Investment) of giving.*

Giving Challenge

Mark May 15 on your calendar, and the next time it rolls around, find a way to say thank-you to the police officers in your community.

I would also love for you to share with me a time when you gave freely with no expectations of anything in return and you received an unexpected gift in return. Go to my Facebook page, www.facebook. com/GivingGal, or send me an e-mail at stephanie@GivingGal. com. Your story may be featured in my blog or a future book!

_____

_____

_____

_____

_____

Day 35: Impact Women's Fund

Introduced in 2007, Impact Porter County, an active giving circle through the Porter County Community Foundation, was created by a group of women who wanted to help other women in the community reach their full potential. The mission of Impact Porter County is to empower women to dramatically improve their lives by collectively funding significant grants that make a lasting impact. Each year women are invited to support the mission with an Impact contribution to the Women's Fund. The goal is simple yet ambitious: raise $100,000 annually, half of which is given away each year in two high-impact grants to advance women in Porter County; half is endowed through the Women's Fund at the Porter County Community Foundation to continue helping women forever.

Never doubt that a small group of thoughtful committed citizens can change the world; indeed, it's the only thing that ever has.

—Margaret Mead

I was invited to the Annual Women's Tea. The tea is the only fundraiser the group hosts all year, and within one hour, the foundation raises over $100,000 to organizations for innovative educational and training programs that are designed to build self-esteem, provide access to women's health services, and promote healthy and safe lifestyles for children and families. I not only gave a donation to show financial support, but it was also a way to get involved in my community and meet new people. (https://www.portercountyfoundation.org/donors/special-donor-groups/impact-porter-county.html)

Giving Challenge

Do you have a community foundation in your county? If you aren't sure, check out http://www.cof.org/community-foundation-locator. Call and learn how you can get involved! If you can't give financially, take time to gain knowledge about the organization, who they are, and what they do. I'm sure you'll find many ways to give.

_____

_____

_____

_____

_____

Day 36: An Empty Seat

Sitting by himself at Moose Tooth Brewing Company, I wondered if he could feel my stares. I was in Alaska, with a cool company Paradigm Shift, to volunteer and speak on giving at a 20 Leadership Camp they were leading for high school and college students. Surrounded by new friends, laughs and smiles everywhere, I was distracted, continually glancing at the guy in the booth next to me. My heart raced and hands sweated. I knew what I needed to do, but I was scared. Questions pinged around in my head. "Will they think I'm doing this because I've preached about giving all week?" "Would he think I'm strange and not want me to sit down?" "If I did approach him, what would I say? 'Hey, you look lonely. Can I sit with you?'"

I felt overwhelmed that something bigger than me was compelling me to go sit with this stranger. Praying for courage, none came. Or maybe it was there but I was ignoring it.

In an attempt to find courage I stood, but instead of introducing myself I walked to the restroom. When I returned, the red scarf wrapped around his neck caught my eye. No longer in control of the direction of my feet, I glided next to his table, extended my hand, stumbling and fumbling with words, and blurted out, "I love your scarf. Red is one of my favorite colors."

Was that it? Was that all I had? What should I do now? I wanted to go back to my seat because I had made an idiot of myself, but the next words out of my mouth surprised me. "May I sit with you?"

A smile gradually filled his face, and with his hand pointing to the empty seat, I sat down. We swapped stories of why I was in Alaska and what brought him to *the last frontier*. A new friendship, even for a moment in time, sprouted.

Out of the corner of my eye, I noticed my group getting restless and people adorning their coats. As I wrapped up our conversation, he reached for his iPad and said, "May I share a project with you?"

"Sure," I said.

Logging into his Facebook page, he pulled up pictures of something that looked very familiar to me. My sixth grade teacher, Roxanne Meyer, had posted similar pictures a few weeks earlier. It was a picture of a Little Free Library®. She had one built-in memory of her friend Candy Wehr and placed it at the local ballpark for the community to enjoy.

He proudly showed me pictures of the gift he had created for the children in his community. He located the library at the bus stop so it would be easily accessible to the children. He fills it with books and swaps them out regularly. He also likes to include books native to Alaska.

Little Free Library's are wood boxes (created to look like schoolhouses), filled with books, placed on a post in a community with a sign "Free Books—Take a Book, Leave a Book."

After looking at his pictures and wrapping up our discussion about Little Free Library, we exchanged names and hugs.

I joined my group and smiled the remainder of the evening. A fellow giver had made my night.

The gift of literacy and access to books is one that will have a ripple effect in the lives of those in his community. God, bless Rufus and his giving spirit.

Giving Challenge

Build or support a Little Free Library® (www.littlefreelibrary.org) in your community.

_____

_____

_____

_____

_____

Day 37: Home Sweet Home

Checking my bags in for a flight, I overheard a frustrated soldier explaining to the attendant his one and only desire: to get home to his family. He had been gone for over a year, had flown around the world, and was one stop away from a glorious reunion with friends and family, specifically mentioning his mom. Picture his mom praying day and night for her son's safe return and that he is on US soil. Her car keys in the ignition waiting for the call to come pick him up and pulling up to the loading area, seeing him exiting the doors of the airport. A moment that has flashed in her mind a million times over the last year.

My heart ached for him. What could I do to help? What would you do?

Leaning over and apologizing for being nosy, looking at the attendant and thinking my husband was going to kill me, I said, "What can I do to get this soldier home to his family? What's it going to cost?"

Shocked and stunned, the soldier said, "No, no, no. I couldn't accept your money. Thank you though."

After a brief discussion, I learned that money wouldn't help. There were no seats available, and someone would have to give up their seat for this young man to make it home sooner than later. I wished he would have been on my flight, as I would have given my seat up in a heartbeat to make sure this soldier made it home.

I thanked him for his service and went along my way. Moments later, I was enjoying lunch and there was the soldier—heading my way.

"Ma'am, thank you so much for trying to help me get home. I really appreciate it."

Tearing up, I said what we all want to say to our soldiers. "No thank you needed. Thank you for your service. Thank you for my freedom." He shook my hand, and as quickly as he approached, he was gone.

Think about the gift our service men and women give us on a daily basis. No flight home, care package, paid dinner, hugs, or thank-you will ever be enough, but we should never stop trying to give thanks.

Can you imagine being gone from home for six months, a year, or longer? How would you feel about not seeing your loved ones on a daily basis? If you are a spouse or parent of a member of our armed forces, you know the feeling. A feeling beyond words.

My friend Todd shared with me the following when I asked him about the sacrifices he has to make to serve our country. He is active in the navy and has served our country for many years.

* * *

"Time away from my wife and kids definitely tops the list of sacrifices. And I'm not referring to my perspective of being away from them and missing them. I am referring to the sacrifice that the family incurs as a whole. To me, family is the ultimate team. When my military obligations have me away from home, the rest of the family has to rally around each other to make sure things stay on track. My incredible wife, Tammy, is suddenly solely responsible for the entire household, not to mention other things, such as law school and a job. Time is invaluable, and it is very hard to not be present at times. Missing out on the opportunity to parent my kids through certain life situations or not be able to attend activities the kids are involved with, etc. It is difficult as a father. Overall, I hope my kids have the ability to understand the big picture, why our military is critical to our well-being, and ultimately I hope the influence I have on them carries over into their decision-making when I cannot be there. But I'm not complaining. I wouldn't change a thing."

Giving Challenge

Do you have a friend who has served or is currently serving in the military? Jot down a couple of ideas below regarding how you could thank them for their service. It may be a dinner out, babysitting their children so they can have a date night with their spouse, or making a connection for them if they need a job. The list is endless of ways we can say thank-you for our freedom.

_____

_____

_____

_____

_____

Day 38: A Card and a Calling

In 2009, my friend Jeni attended a Christ in Youth conference. During the conference, organizers passed around sealed envelopes to the youth in the audience. The envelopes contained challenges for the teenagers to serve someone other than themselves. Adults were encouraged to take the cards, but they didn't have to. If you know my friend Jeni, there wasn't a doubt that she would pass up a card. Here's the rest of the story.

Jeni prayed and felt God tugging on her heart to open the envelope. She slipped a card out and it read, "500 Turkeys. Raise enough food and funds to feed 500 families for Thanksgiving."

Wow! Can you imagine opening the envelope and pulling out that card? I'm pretty sure I would be jamming the card back in and find some tape to reseal.

But that is not what Jeni did. She came home and started planning and organizing, and in 2009, she met her goal of feeding five hundred families. From 2009 to 2015, 500 Turkeys, now an official nonprofit, has provided meals for over 4,700 families.

She said, "God didn't just put this mission on me. It took an entire community to feed a community. People learn that it's easy to help other people. That is spawns off to other people helping their communities. It isn't about 500 Turkeys itself. It is about people learning you can do more for your community; you can help your neighborhood, or a kid in your school. 500 Turkeys has certainly impacted my life. I stand back sometimes and I watch in awe of the incredible miracles God has put in front of us that sometimes I'm not sure I can take it in. It's an absolute blessing to be able to do it. It's really easy to help someone in need."

Giving Challenge

I'm not going to challenge you to feed five hundred families. But if you feel called to do it, go for it! I challenge you to do something nice for the Jenis of the world. They give selflessly of their time and talents. Send a note of encouragement, gather a group of friends and go in on massage gift certificate, or send a box of chocolates! No matter the size, people love to be appreciated and recognized for the works they do, even though most don't do it for those purposes.

_____

_____

_____

_____

_____

Day 39: Make a Difference to Someone Today

Written by: Deanna Day Young

Today (January 27) is my sister's birthday. She would have been forty-seven. She suffered with cancer for nine years and gave up the long fight in December 2014.

She loved doing things for other people. That is why it seemed appropriate to take the idea of Bucket Buddies Mission and incorporate it in her honor a few months before she died. The mission statement for Bucket Buddies Mission, Inc. is to make a difference to children suffering from cancer and other life-threatening conditions by showing the love of Christ through providing gift buckets of kindness to children. It provides gift buckets to children with cancer and other life-threatening illnesses who are patients in hospitals and other settings. The buckets may include items such as coloring books, crayons, small toys, playing cards, journals, pens, fingernail polish, toy cars, and word search books. There is no cost to the hospital or the patient. It is a gift from Bucket Buddies Mission, Inc.

We have been blessed to have delivered over 2,500 buckets to fourteen states plus Canada in just a little over a year and a half. Hill-Rom, Inc. offered employees across its locations in North America an opportunity to volunteer for this organization, and we had an overwhelming response. In just one day, volunteers filled over 1,300 buckets in seven states and Canada and delivered to twelve hospitals or facilities and made a difference too many children.

www.BucketBuddiesMission.org

Giving Challenge

Deanna is a good friend of mine. She has taken a tragedy and turned it into a non-profit to help thousands of children. With a little motivation and a hard work ethic anyone can make a difference, one person at a time.

In memory of a loved one, I encourage you to do something to make a difference to someone: flash a smile, buy someone a cup of coffee, pass up a good parking spot, send a bouquet of flowers, etc. If we all do something kind today, we'll change the world.

_____

_____

_____

_____

_____

Day 40: They Call Me Mom

Sitting on the airplane to Anchorage, Alaska, I didn't realize how my life was about to change forever. In 2014 I met a couple of guys, Jerrod and Ryan, on the Internet, joined their Live Your List Facebook group, and the next thing I knew, I was headed to Alaska to participate in and speak at a 20 Leadership Camp. Crazy, crazy, crazy!

I was the oldest one in the group. The leader was four years younger than me, and the rest … Well, yes, I was old enough to be their mom. I had trouble processing the thought at first. How did I get so old? How was it possible that if I had children, one could be in college right now?

The girls' sleeping quarters were at a different location from the guys. This old lady—okay, I'm only thirty-nine—had intentions of getting rest on this trip, as it was my "vacation" from work. The "girlies," as we refer to each other, had other plans for me. Each night they'd pile into my bed and keep me up talking about whatever girls talk about. I think I got six hours of sleep total in the last three days. I don't remember being this exhausted in college.

Within a couple of days, the girls were calling me "Mom." It was a word I thought I would never hear said in reference to me. During prayer time, I realized that I didn't need to physically birth these girls to be a mother figure in their lives. Even though all three had wonderful, loving mothers, God knew there was a role I needed to play in their lives.

It's been several months since my Alaskan adventure, and I feel as if "my girls"—Jessica, Shelby, and Toshali—have been in my life forever. Was there life before them? They Facebook message and text me all hours of the day, send me things in the mail (and I do the same), and we've committed Sunday evenings to video calls. I'm sad when our calls end. We've planned trips to see each other, share with each other our dreams, and hold each other accountable for weekly goals.

My life is busy. Very busy. And if you would have told me in December 2015 I'd have time to invest in three girls, I would have said you were crazy! But guess what? When God has other plans, you reprioritize, you make sacrifices, and you find time to invest in the future generation.

Giving Challenge

Someone you know is struggling with infertility. They have dreams of having and holding a child of their own. That someone may be you. I pray their prayers are answered. But if children is not in the cards, I hope they don't wish time away. Live life, invest in others, and find a teenager who needs a friend or a college student that needs a second "mom." I think back to my childhood and I had the most amazing mom, but I was also surrounded by many women who invested in me and played a role in making me who I am today. One of the greatest mothers of all time—Mother Teresa—said, "A life not lived for others is not a life."

Your Turn! Start Giving Today!

Thank you! Thank you for letting me share forty of my favorite giving stories with you. My giving journey began more than five years ago, and now as I sit here writing, I'm still challenging myself to look for new opportunities to simply give every day. Giving has become an instinct, a part of who I am at my core. In the beginning, I thought *I* was the one giving gifts, but I quickly learned the old adage is true. "The more you give, the more you get."

During my giving journey, I was contacted by a lady who stumbled upon my blog and started to follow my gift-giving journey. She had many questions about how I got started and decided what gifts to give. I love hearing from fellow givers, whether a beginner or lifelong giver. Getting to talk to new people and make personal connections is even better.

I let this woman know I had read *29 Gifts* and that it motivated me to start giving, and not just for twenty-nine days, but for an entire year. That year made such an impact in my life that I continued into a second year. I explained to her that in the beginning, gifts were sometimes hard to come by and many days I relied on creativity and seeking out opportunities. But as the days, weeks, and months went by, opportunities began presenting themselves and the gift giving became a daily habit.

I checked in with this young lady at the end of her first month and she gave me permission to share her response and experience. Here it is:

Hi Stephanie. I am so excited to tell you about my twenty-nine days that unintentionally has turned into thirty-one and going. Well, it hasn't been easy, but it has been interesting and very surprising. I found that on every single occasion that I gave something, I got something in return. This was not my intention whatsoever, but I have received an award for every act.

The most interesting incidence of giving happened one day when I was frustrated and very upset and couldn't focus on something to give. So I took an idea from you and while I was running errands, I drove through a drive-thru and purchased a coffee drink—and of course paid for the car behind me. On my way home, I noticed the same car behind me. I didn't think anything of it, but then I actually started to wonder if I had offended the driver somehow.

Well, she followed me home. I got out of my car ready to apologize when an old friend popped out of her car and thanked me for the coffee and wanted to know why I hadn't just waved her down so we could have coffee together. I had no idea I knew the person. It has been a few years, I didn't recognize the car, and I deliberately didn't look in my rearview mirror, because for some reason this particular act made me nervous.

Another beautiful thing I am finding is that every time I talk about this with family and friends, I get more "leads," if you will, for giving, and others are considering a journey of their own.

On day 29 an acquaintance asked me to provide them some consultative services for a fee. I volunteered my effort—that leads to a nice contract for the spring. Completely unexpected but very cool!

I have continued with days 30 and 31 and will keep going. I do think it is a habit now, another reward for me.

So when I started, I did not expect rewards. It is strange. I love giving and in the past over thought things so much that when I gave, the recipient often felt like they had to give something back to me, which was very uncomfortable for both of us. This journey, while I think about it every single day, has made things so much easier in that the gifts are simple, unpretentious, and don't render that feeling of obligation on anyone's part.

So glad I caught your blog on this! It doesn't matter if my gifts are even acknowledged by the recipients or if I even know who directly benefits. I think the practice of just giving changes so many things we can't be aware of unless we make the effort.

Will You Take the Challenge?

I hope this young lady's and my stories inspire you to start your own gift-giving journey. I request the following:

- Take this amazing adventure for forty days. Set a goal to give a gift for a day, a week, or a month. It's a start! I can almost guarantee it will not only become a habit but a also lifestyle that will change your life and the lives of those around you. The more you give, the more generous you will be with your time, money, talents, and possessions.

- Share this book with friends and family, encourage them it read it, and share with others.

- If you enjoyed the book, I'd love if you would write a review on Amazon or GoodReads

- Share your "Giving Challenge" with me via social media and tag #GivingChallenge or e-mail.

- Share your giving story with me to possibly be featured on my blog, social medial, or a future book.

- Follow me on social media to find more "Giving Challenges."

Sign up for my forty-day giving challenge and get twelve bonus stories at www.theGivingChallenge.co.

Blog: GivingGal.com

Twitter: @Giving_Gal

Facebook: facebook.com/GivingGal

Pinterest: Pinterest.com/Giving_Gal

Instagram: Giving_Gal

I love speaking on the topic of giving. If you need a speaker for your conference, church service, retreat or workshop, I'm your gal!

If you have questions, want to share a story, or need giving ideas, drop me an e-mail at Stephanie@GivingGal.com.

I'd love to hear from you!

Blessings, Stephanie

Acknowledgments

I have to start off by thanking God for blessing me beyond my imagination. I thank God for bringing amazing people into my life and tapping me on the shoulder, every so often, and whispering in my ear to help a stranger.

I also have to thank following people:

My husband, for staying on me to get this book finished and supporting me every day on my giving journey.

My parents, who didn't just tell me about helping others while growing up but showed me day in and day out through their actions.

Cortney and Doug, for being an inspiration in taking a mission laid on your heart and turning it into a reality with their nonprofit Giving Hearts a Hand.

Josie, Nathan, Carson and Ella, who always teach me you are never too young to learn about giving and getting involved. Even at a young age, you show eagerness to volunteer and help others.

Angela Connor, for reading my first draft and providing honest feedback. Ken and Ron, owners of Three Oaks Inn, for providing me a haven to finish my stories. Kerrie Hora and Rebecca Shellito, for being my soul sisters and holding me accountable to getting this book completed. Barb Young, for the encouraging letter you wrote me several years ago. You had confidence in me that I didn't have in myself. Ann Bowman, for your encouragement and love of books and reading. I treasure our chats about both. Jeannie Nowarita, for meeting me at Starbucks on Monday nights to jump-start my writing.

My development editor, Anna Floit, at the Peacock Quill. I couldn't have completed this project without you. I not only gained an editor but also a friend.

Michelle Pendergrass, editor and friend. Thank you for your input and your patience. You took my jumbled words and made my dream a reality. I'm so glad you followed your passion for painting. If you hadn't, we may have never met.

Cisco, I'm proud to work for a company that provides matching funds for employee donations and gives employees five paid days off to give back. It leads by example and is involved in numerous giving-back efforts around the world.

My dear friends of the Pursuit Mastermind (Kelsey, Whitney, Amy, and Jessica), *Live Your List*, *LaunchOut*, *30 Days of Hustle*, and *Dreamers and Builders*. You have all been of tremendous encouragement and inspiration. You continue to remind me that dreaming big is okay and anything is possible. As Willy Wonka said, "We are the music makers and we are the dreamers of dreams."

Resources

Adoption: www.showhope.org

Bucket Buddies: www.BucketBuddiesMission.org.

Clearance: Buy candy, cards, hat, gloves, and more off-season. Always check out the clearance section.

Community Foundation Locator: http://www.cof.org/community-foundation-locator.

Dollar Tree can meet many of your gift-giving needs, from cards and wrapping paper to stickers, toys, and books.

Giving Hearts a Hand: http://givingheartsahand.org/.

Kiwanis: This global organization of volunteers is dedicated to improving the world, one child and one community at a time. http://www.kiwanis.org/.

Little Free Library: www.littlefreelibrary.org.

Operation Christmas Child: www.samaritanspurse.org/occ.

Rice Bowls: www.RiceBowls.org

Soles4Souls: To learn more about Soles4Souls and how to donate new or used shoes to http://www.soles4souls.org.

United Way: www.unitedway.org.

Notes